SONGS
FROM A
UNIVERSE

THE POETRY OF
MICHAEL GRAVES

SONGS FROM A UNIVERSE

Copyright 2024 Michael Graves

All Rights Reserved.

No part of this book may be reproduced or transmitted in any form or by any means electronic or mechanical including photocopying, recording, or by any information storage and retrieval system without written permission from the copyright holder.

ISBN: 978-1-948261-82-1

Library of Congress Control Number:

Cover and Interior Design: Diane Woods

www.dianewoodsdesign.com

Published 2024 by Hugo House Publishers, Ltd.
Denver, Colorado   Austin, Texas

DEDICATION

I have written this book to you.
I don't know the masses of people out there
and I can't speak to them;
nor would I attempt to.
But I do feel like I know you.

This entire lifetime I have worked to understand
why people do what they do; how they think
And what makes them who they are.

My chosen weapons in this hunt were:
Observation, philosophy and poetry.

Not so much "a philosophy"
although I have used a couple far more than others,
as how philosophy, a love of wisdom, is done.
The math of existence
in a search for a clean perception of truth.

Thank you for sharing my poetry.
I hope that it is helpful to you
and that you can use it to help others.

--Michael Graves 4/7/24

TABLE OF CONTENTS

Songs From a Universe ii
Dedication iii
Table of Contents iv
Art 1
   Homeland 1
   Like Hemingway on The Streets of Spain 5
   Snacking on Bukowski 8
   Steinbeck's Ghost 11
   A Penchant for Strippers 14
   Dancing with the Muse 16
   A Realm of Shattered Time 20
   At the Base of it All 23
   Authenticity 24
   Baby Poet 27
   Chats With Fredric 29
   Departure 30
   Different Doors 32
   Hambone and Bimboface in the Alley (Act V, sc. 1)
   34
   Rising from the Fall from Height 35
   Steel Flower/Concrete Soil 38

"The Blonde"	40
The Life of Dreams	43
The Muse	46
The Perfect Life	47
The Secret Handshake from God	48
This Afternoon the Muse Came to Visit	50
This Moment in Time	52
Weaver	54
When I Go Among People	58
Death and Life	**61**
Mortality	61
Apparency	64
Farewell on a winter night – I will return	66
An Epitaph to Missing Friends . .	68
Waiting for You	71
Funeral for a Friend	75
Humor	**77**
On the Use of the Phrase "You Bastards!"	77
Nose Pickers	79
Nipples	82
Deja Poo	84
On Doing	85
On 'Maybes'	86
Roots	87

The Church of Tits and Ass 88
The End of the World (with slight apologies to John Lennon for playing off of his piece: "Give Peace a Chance.") 93

Immortality **97**

A Movement in the Air 97

Stardust 99

The Dance 101

Tightrope 103

Connecting Dots 105

Actors (Death as a Masquerade) 107

Hide and Seek 109

The Artery 111

Travelers 112

Truth and Death 114

Life **117**

The View from the Lighthouse 117

The Mode of the Hummingbird 120

The Life That You Create 124

Runway 24, Lukla, Nepal 125

6 Secrets: In the Key of Dali 128

A Simple Step 134

An Unwasted Life 135

Angel Rising 137

Barriers to Flight	138
Barriers	140
Beatitudes	144
Brushwork	147
Catch and Release	149
The Cutting Edge of the Blade	151
Darkness and Light	153
Decision	155
Definition	157
Distraction	159
Doorways	160
Dreams - (in four short acts)	162
Eight Couplets: A Reminder	165
Heroes (To Erin)	166
Inner Voice	168
Integrity	169
Intention	171
Kingdom of Dreams	172
Life as a Human	173
Life is not a Death Sentence	174
On the observation of a cripple, yet buoyant.	175
Path	176
Quality	177
Radiance	179

Recipe (This is for you - today) 181
The Seeds of Illusions 183
Slicing Tomatoes 185
Space 186
Stuck 188
Taking Off My Watch 190
Thanksgiving 191
The Cliff 195
The Mirror 197
The New Year -- Angel Falls 199
The Past 201
The Taken Road 203
Version 6.1 204
Wake-up Call 208
Prescience 209

The Vincent Series 211

The Unquiet Mind (Vincent No. 1) 211
The Night is Still (Vincent No. 2) 216
The Focus of Madness – (Vincent No. 3) 219
Wheatfield with Crows (Vincent No. 4) 224
Epilogue (Vincent No. 5 – Van Gogh did not kill himself) 228

Love 235

The Secret to Good Sex (a modified sonnet*) 235

Woman	238
The River	240
The Whisper of Sheets	242
This Morning I Stayed in Bed (for Holley)	244
Love Match	246
Again . . . (A love song)	250
Beauty	252
Courtney	253
Crystalline -- A love story in three small parts	255
Erin	258
Eye of the Beholder	259
"Gerunds, Verbs, a Couple of Adjectives and an Adverb"	261
I Loved You More	265
Last Night in Houston	266
Lingerie	268
Merchants of Small Wars	269
Missing Pieces	272
Mountaineer (to Jaxon)	274
Pre-Houston Rush	277
Road Map	278
The Sidelong Glance	279
Smile Today	281
Sunday Morning Interruptus	282

The Air	283
The Buoy	284
The Fool/The Blindness	287
The Sea	290
Tips From My Father	293
Today I go to take back Houston	294
Tonight	296
Travel Guide	297
What to Send Railyn and Kiara for Christmas?	298
You were simply gone	300
Magic	**303**
Reminder: Magic	303
Life's a Mystery	305
Questions	**307**
Why Are We Here?	307
Musica Proxima Etern*	310
Travel: In-between the Ticks of Time	312
The Easy Answer	315
Why we do what we do	318
A Little Ado About Nothing	321
Aliens're Comin'!	323
Angel Wings	328
Breathing	331
Farside Traveler	335

Gaia (Clues to Existence) 337
Gaia* Rising 343
Geography 347
God is a Mirror 349
I am not my chair 350
Messages in a Bottle 353
Ollantaytambo 361
Point of View: Escape Velocity 367
Sailing (Song of the Daemons*) 370
Simplicity 373
Spiderwebs and Evolution 375
The Dahlia 381
The Root of Strength 382
Visitor 384

Social Responsibility 387
America 2197 387
Friendship 393
Mother is Listening 397
The Belly of the Beast 399
Vengeance *'lex talionis'* (For the suicide bombers) 402
Watch Me 405
The Vengeance of Angels 406
A Few Words on the Study of Philosophy 407
A Red Horse in a Fallow Field 411

All Lives Matter	415
America: The Election Year	420
Bricks	423
Circumstance	426
Detergent	429
Don't	430
God: Getting Bored . . .	431
How to Cook a Frog	435
In killing me . . .	436
Maniac (for Syria)	437
On Social Media	441
Poseurs	443
Superhuman Monkeys (Song Lyrics)	445
Tahrir Square -- The Beginning	448
Take a Drug	455
Terrorist	459
The Evil White Male	460
The Fixed Game	463
The Gardener	465
The Hatred of the Rich	468
The Owl	471
They Went	472
TV Newscasters	473
We Should be More Than Just Entertainment	474

On Poetry and Social Responsibility 477
"Night Must Fall on the Regime" 480
Writing - Poetry 487
Poetic Convergence 487
The Poet's Spell 491
Regarding Editing 498
Borders is Closing (A Saturday afternoon; and the passing of a friend.) 499
Just Because 502
On Writing - a note to Paul W. Morris Sr. in 2012 505
Something that Rhymes - On the "Importance" of Rhyming 509
The Poet 510
A Poet's Wish 512

ART

Homeland

I live in a land that lies between
Ars Poetica and Daylight.
Near Poesia the sea of dreams
shining softly in the moonlight.

'cross the Isthmus of Illusion, down
the River of Riotous Times.
You'll find me there, beneath a tree
happily batting out rhymes.

Beyond the Plains of Perilous Plight
and the Hills of Recombinant Verse.
It's a land where poetry lingers like clouds
in a sky you'd just love to traverse;

in a huge balloon made of phrases and verbs
tied together with lines of conjunction.
Buoyed by verses so light and so clear
so delightful they near' restrict function.

On the other hand, there's another land
to the east, where the verse is so sodden
that poets (who normally are creatures of light) are
quite proud of being downtrodden.

In Pedantia, poetry's a serious thing
made with scary rules and compunction.
With so many levels of interpretation
you can barely retain mental function.

With references so arcane and obscure
that it's easy to question validity.
Except when you note that the poet who wrote them
died drowning in excess perfidy.

Clarity in poetry's a dangerous thing
that terrifies scholars and hokes
who, failing to see to the bottom of things
bind their words up in mirrors and smoke.

The effortless flow of simplicity, just
evades their awareness, I guess.
And all they intend, at the end of it all
is to wow and confuse and impress.

But the poetry of truth can be simple and clear
without so much as a riddle.
Its premise is such that it needs no device
no artifice nor tremulous fiddl(ing).

A poetic statement, clear and concise
understood by any who read it
is vastly superior to one made with lines
so confusing they act to defeat it.

A piece thickly bound in pedantics
based on overworked pontification
makes a far better sermon, than poetic verse
as it's rooted in obfuscation.

My homeland though, is in a place
where poetry's thankfully brimming
with lightness and grace, laid out at a pace
that doesn't set your head spinning.

I come from a land that lies between
Ars Poetica and Daylight.
Near Poesia, the sea of dreams
shining softly in the moonlight.

'cross the Isthmus of Illusion, down
the River of Riotous Times.
You'll find me here at the end of my days
happily batting out rhymes.

     --Graves 9/22/12

Notes:
Ars Poetica: Ars Poetica is a term meaning "The Art of Poetry" or "On the Nature of Poetry". Early examples of Artes Poeticae by Aristotle and Horace have survived and many other poems bear the same name.

Poesia: Italian/Portuguese: Poetry

Pedantica: A fictional land; from Pedantic: "Characterized by a narrow, often ostentatious concern for book learning and formal rules. Marked by a narrow, often tiresome focus on or display of learning, and especially its trivial aspects."

hoke: One who hokes or "hokes up". Originally from "hokum", "to hoke", means: "to alter or manipulate so as to give a deceptively or superficially improved quality or value (usually followed by up): as in: "a political speech hoked up with phony statistics." One who hokes things up, is therefore a "hoke."

Like Hemingway on The Streets of Spain

The road stretches long and empty
when the Muse leaves.

The heart aches to capacity, and then overflows
with emptiness.
The wooden palette lays
against the wall, stained
with faded pigment:
A brittle, hollow gourd, once filled with unending
rapacious inspiration and promises

of a future where
creation is as effortless as the sparking
of two ideas moving together in the wet, sultry night.

Water is not coming.
There is no quenching the thirst at
the death of the soul.

I sit and remember times
when life was much like
Hemingway on the streets of Spain. Walking
the cobblestones of Pamplona, already working
on "Death in the Afternoon."

The pulse of life pounding. Coursing with
the weight and texture of that which falls
with night and rises with the streaming
bleeding color of the new day.
And which finally ends
when she leaves
for the last time.

Now, at the end, the winds
of the Pyrenees scrub
the air of Pamplona clean
of the foul smell of blood.
The roar of the crowd has gone home, and
the bloodlust (having served its purpose) is politely
folded and placed back into pockets and
purses, like some used, dirty handkerchief to be taken
home and laundered clean in private.
To be reborn in a pristine state.
As though this could hide its nature.

The carcasses of the fallen
have been hauled away
leaving only drag-marks in the dirt; baking
in the languid afternoon.

The matador, so proud of his cheap rhinestones
hums a small tune of the bullfight
tightens his borrowed mask, and
leans back on a thin, unsteady, green chair
in the shadow of the crowded cafe.
He tunes his small guitar sharp from flat.
Waiting for the attention he considers
his due; now that the "noble"
slaughter is over.

The hands of beggars in the
red-dirt road that leads elsewhere, are
lined from overwork
clutching at the air
hoping to get her attention
in the end, fatally
unaware that
the only way
to attract the Muse
is to continue to create.

       -- Graves 12/30/14

Snacking on Bukowski

I go to the bookstore because
I'm hungry. Because I miss
the taste of air that's been slowly
seasoned, with thousands of books.

Because I need to sit in a place
with a thousand, thousand doors
that open into the labyrinthine minds
of a thousand, thousand artists.

A place with endless lines
of ink, spilling onto pages in
orderly rows; belying
the wild, raving
luscious canvas within.

A place where staid black and white, blend
to create brighter and more vivid
colors than those that see
the light of day.

Because I need to run my fingers
slowly
down soft
spines
of beautiful stories, wishing
I had time to do them all.
My imagination snacking
on candy.

I wander.
I breathe.
I breathe.
My insides relax.
I feel the texture of paper
slick as the ice in Spring
or formed from tiny chunks of trees
otherwise left forgotten.

I crack open Bukowski and read the short, broken
lines, slipping down
the textured page.
Just a snack.
(He's always there.)
Until I realize I have to go.
Realize that I've been
smiling the entire time.
And Charles has reminded me
how much I like to read.

--Graves 12/30/14

Note: Charles Bukowski (August 16, 1920 – March 9, 1994) was a German-born American poet, novelist and short story writer. His work addresses the ordinary lives of poor Americans in Los Angeles, the city where he lived and which provided the background for his inspiration. Bukowski wrote thousands of poems, hundreds of short stories and six novels, eventually publishing over sixty books.

The FBI kept a file on him as a result of his column, "Notes of a Dirty Old Man," published in the LA underground newspaper "Open City." In 1986 Time Magazine called Bukowski a "laureate of American lowlife".

Bukowski's gravestone reads: "Don't Try," a phrase which he uses in one of his poems, advising aspiring writers and poets about inspiration and creativity. Bukowski explained the phrase in a 1963 letter to John William Corrington: "Somebody at one of these places [...] asked me: 'What do you do? How do you write, create?' You don't, I told them. You don't try. That's very important: not to try, either for Cadillacs, creation or immortality. You wait, and if nothing happens, you wait some more. It's like a bug high on the wall. You wait for it to come to you. When it gets close enough you reach out, slap out and kill it. Or if you like its looks, you make a pet out of it."

Steinbeck's Ghost

Steinbeck walks the short, straight streets among
the weather-worn, wooden walls of Cannery Row
swapping jokes with Ed Ricketts, each
out-shouting the bashing, booming waves.
Laughing like two men sharing the last drink
before the bottle breaks into flying, sparkling splinters
on the rocks that edge the bay.

Back-slapping they wander
planning the trip to British Columbia to
write "The Outer Shores."
Ed, living for tidepool discoveries
on the gray, windy edge of
Monterey Bay.
John pinching Carol.
Pounding out psalms of the displaced.
Etching the glass of humanity with
hard lines from a bindlestiff's memory.
Cutting glass with an
Hermes Baby portable typewriter
in the foggy, fecund air of
the Pajaro Valley. Carving
his way into the consciousness
of America with
diamond-hard tales of the wandering underclass.

A wanderlust, less lust than hunger
and the need to keep moving.
For to stop is to court the stillness
of death. To face the fear of the fatality of roots
that tie the wandering soul to the earth and
frame the grave which awaits the stationary man.

Even now, he pounds
in the noisy stillness
amid the roar of gray, autumn waves.
Cutting glass with an
Hermes Baby portable typewriter
in the foggy, fecund air of
the Pajaro Valley.
Dead for forty years.

     --Graves 4/9/17

Notes:

Cannery Row is a waterfront street in Monterey, California that was the setting of John Steinbeck's novels *"Cannery Row"* and *"Sweet Thursday."* Formerly a nickname for Ocean View Avenue, which was lined by a number of now-defunct sardine canning factories; the name of the street was officially changed to Cannery Row in 1958 to honor Steinbeck. In the opening sentence of *Cannery Row*, Steinbeck describes the street as "a poem, a stink, a grating noise, a quality of light, a tone, a habit, a nostalgia, a dream."

Ed Ricketts was the inspiration for several characters in Steinbeck's novels. He met then-aspiring writer John Steinbeck in late 1930, shortly after Steinbeck and his wife Carol moved to Pacific Grove, California. Carol worked part-time for Ricketts at *Pacific Biological Laboratories*, his biological supply house and lab, for about a year. Steinbeck who lived near the lab, spent time there, learning marine biology, helping Ricketts preserve specimens and talking about philosophy. They remained good friends for the rest of their lives. The remains of *Pacific Biological Laboratories*, are preserved in their original location at 800 Cannery Row in Monterey.

Hermes Baby typewriter: A compact, Swiss-built portable typewriter that was a favorite among writers of the 1940's due to its precision engineering. It was billed by the company as "the worlds lightest portable typewriter" and was called "the ideal typewriter for students, occasional typists and people on the road."

Pajaro Valley, California: Located on the Central California Coast, the Pajaro Valley runs from the Coast Mountain Range to Monterey Bay. It is home to some of the most fertile farmland in the world.

A Penchant for Strippers

Life moves like a dancer, lithely wrapping
herself around opportunity with
the fluid grace of flowing time. Beckoning
and teasing in ways as old
as the cold void between the
pulsing heat of stars.

She stirs the hunger that
draws things out of hiding;
squeezing dreams
out of possibility. Anticipation
bred of implication.
Beauty in unanticipated
flashes, in the light
of darkened places.

I've always had a penchant for strippers
so to speak.
Life is like that. I've always
been a bit bemused by
people who are scared
to look at the beauty in life
that is clearly there to be seen
and drink it in.

They look
but with furtive glances. Stares
purposefully averted, as from
a beautiful book on a shelf, never
opened for fear of wrinkling its pages.
A compass, fixed anxiously
on the mundane. Fearful
of leaving the comfort
of the harbor – not knowing
what now lies ahead –
for fear of a joy
from which they cannot
withdraw. A joy that may
disturb the calm surface of
their small pond.

Fear that they may have to carry
some new vision, alone. That they
may stumble under the
weight of that load.

Better to not see.

So much to fear.

And all the while
life beckons and whirls, flashing
mysteries to be plumbed; delights
to be seen; wonders to
be unfolded with your fingers
like the fresh petals of the
first bloom in spring.

     –Graves 2/6/16

Dancing with the Muse

There's something you have to
understand about dancing
with the Muse.

Nothing else

can touch
the soul-subsuming exhilaration
of the dance.
Nothing.

But it can also be fatal.

Ask Hemingway or Poe
(or a few hundred others)
and they'll tell you:
"The Muse takes no prisoners."

She will bring you
to places you have never been
then she'll dump you out
and leave you to find your own way back.

And you will sit
and wait for her return
like some strung-out
lover, waiting by the phone
for a call. And the waiting

tear out
your heart.

This was Ernie's problem, in the end.
Edgar's, too.
It's no mystery
if you've danced.

When I first danced
(truly danced) with the Muse
I never wanted to return
to the world.

She brought me to see things
I had never
seen. Drew out
expressions I had never
before imagined, as she
consumed me, bit by bit, with
the burning, holy fire.

And she left me
with an empty
craving hunger for creation
as she has with so many others (the whore).

Each of them grateful to be chosen
even while watching the erection
piece-by-piece
of the guillotine
at the end of this road.

The only way to beat the Muse
is to dance with her, and never
fail to lead.
You must drive your art.
You can't let it drive you.

Just because the guillotine is built
does not mean
that your name has been
indelibly etched
upon the blade.

She is the most impressive
of the figures of the dance.
For there are truly
"none like [her] among the dancers,
None with swift feet."
None who cause the heart
to Pound.
None who balance quite so well
on motes drifting in the
sunlight shaft that penetrates
the darkened room.

You must lead.
And if you do, the Muse will follow
so adroitly that all
you notice is
the lightness
of the pas de deux.

–Graves 9/7/18

Note:
The quote "none like [her] among the dancers,
None with swift feet," was taken from "*Dance Figure*" by Ezra Pound.

A Realm of Shattered Time

(To Leonard Cohen – on hearing of his passing)

I remember when you first sang to me
of Suzanne and of the river.
I heard your voice crawl forth like some
massive tree - growing from
the bottom of a deep, hollow
well - searching for water.

You bid farewell to Marianne
sang Hallelujah in the darkened night.
And promised in poetic verse, that
I'd be hearing from you
long after you're gone. Long
after the river widened
beyond the point of passing.

You walked the narrow edge of heights;
the long-game in which
the words are not complete
until they're done. Though crafting
carries on for years.

You were there before us. And you
will be there, long
after we're gone.
A light in the darkness.
An icon against which to measure
the critical balance of content
in terms of discontent, albeit with a perfection
which nonetheless creaks with the strain
of being human.

And now, although they say you're gone
if I listen carefully in the empty night
I can hear you coughing
a hundred floors above me
in the Tower of Song.

             – Graves 2/21/20

Note: Originally written 11/13/16

Leonard Cohen (Sept. 21, 1934 – Nov 7, 2016): Canadian poet, songwriter, painter, novelist. His words shaped the artistic development of many of the top songwriters and poets of the five decades spanning 1967 with the launch of his first album (Songs of Leonard Cohen) through the launch of his last; three weeks before his death in 2016 (You Want It Darker).

For many, his singing voice was an acquired taste much like Bob Dylan, Janice Joplin, Phil Ochs and a few others. His ability as a poet was exceptional. He wrote many impressive pieces. A sample of just a few that I would commend to you includes: "Hallelujah", "Sisters of Mercy", "Tower of Song", Seems So Long Ago, Nancy", "Farewell Marianne", "Dance Me To The End of Love," "Suzanne" "The Stranger Song." There are more that have been omitted here, than I can count. You may not entirely appreciate his voice, but his lyrics are second to none.

You were never best, I thought
at singing your own stuff
But you were you, and only you
and my friend, that was enough.
– MG

I will miss him.

At the Base of it All

At the base of it all
the artist alone
sees the ravening, soul-cleansing
vision revealed to her by
an often cruelly capricious Muse.

It is the holy crusade to
communicate this reality
which drives art.

> --Graves 1/20/17

Authenticity

The world spreads out
in all directions. Everything
that you do influences
the flow of time. Everything
that you do etches
your presence on the future.

Subjugate your divine sensibilities
to the boundaries of others:
To their tastes,
to their particular beliefs
to their odd notions propriety; and
your own singular, holy
influence on the tides of time
Is tainted - stunted - perverted, and
your message is
stained.

You have
something to say, that
others need to hear.
You have
something to accomplish
which will save
the life of at least
one other.

Do not allow your message
to be blunted by mice, watching
cautiously from the sidelines
apprehensively wringing their hands.
Or perverted by those
cloaked in shadows, leering
as you dance to
their terrible music.
No one ever won by believing in the virtue
of tremulous whispers.
By stooping gratefully before the
dripping axe of a scornful king.

No one ever won anything by
holding back when the
full measure of strength was called for.

Go - Full - Out.
But go as yourself.

Don't do it as
"someone else" who is doing it.
Don't write
as you "think a writer should"
or paint
as you "think a painter would"
or design
in fearful conformity to "the rules."

It's YOUR message!
Say it in your OWN
words! Put the paint
on the medium as YOU
see the message, and

NEVER! live life as it
has been ascribed to you.
Do these things as
you
would do them
as if there were no one
to answer to. For anything
else is to live a shallow death
waiting cautiously
full of second-guesses
for the deep one which brings
your struggling hesitancy
to an end.

It's your shot
this life.
Do it right.

      -Graves 11/15/22

Taken from "Reflections on a Crystal Wind."

Baby Poet

She passes three-lined
notes in class, about
her latest crush. Then
hurriedly posts them to
the web; as though they're
the epiphanies which will
set the collective mind
of the literati on its heels.
Shakespeare and Rumi should
make way.

Graffiti as poetry.
Dashed off and deposited
on Instagram in a blink.

She's very impressed with herself.
All hormones; loosely wrapped
in colored, crinkly tissue paper cliches.
Trite strings of words.
Nothing new here.

At least she writes.

Her experience is a mud puddle.
It has not yet grown into
the deep, raging sea that
it will become. It has not yet
soared the ecstatic
heights it will attain.

She's very impressed
with herself.

She's a baby poet.
I've been there.
I hope she makes it.

     --Graves 9/12/22

Chats With Fredric

Every so often . . .
Every so "once in a long while," I think
that if it were not for Chopin:
The trees would burst apart at the base, in
loud, violent explosions of
sharp, tiny splinters and spring free of the Earth
like rockets. And
the sky would fold in on itself
in a whooshing, roaring, rushing spiral
and disappear down the rabbit hole.

Then, Fredric reaches down;
gathers a handful of rich, brown earth
in his cupped hand, lets it run out
slowly
from between his fingers, and
fall to the ground, just so
to take its rightful place.

And everything is righted.
The tiny, bright stars begin to harmonize
once more.
And I remember where I left my
coffee.

      --Graves 11/4/15

Departure

The Muse lets you down easy, or
the Muse lets you down hard.
But the Muse, invariably
lets you fall.

And leaves you
wondering, Why?
The time, the energy spent
communicating ideas
a plethora of visions.

The reaching out
to change lives.
To bring light.
To show a different
vision; all come to vapors on
the morning wind;
in the swirling colors
of time splashed across
a vanishing canvas which
grants no permanence. Why?

Because somewhere
in someone
you hope to leave
a spark.

Roll the dice.
It ends the same.
But sometimes the ride
is different.

Roll the dice.

                --Graves 11/26/21

Different Doors

Art is a competitive event
only among fools.

Don't concern yourself with those
who create what you do not. No matter
the brilliance of their light.
For they do not create
as you would create.

There is no competition among artists.
There are only different doors.
Other roads.
Windows that open
onto a different land.

The world that you create
is yours. And its vistas
are like no others.

Share it
or not.
It is your decision.
And only yours.

Don't be concerned
that what you create
will be less than that
of another – or more.

For in that direction lies
only death; or worse:
the decision to not create.

You are born of the raging winds
the mirrored pool
and the winding road that never ends.
You reside in that highest place
that looks out on vistas
which only you can see.

You are the only one
who will bring them home.
Or not.
As you decide.

                                        –Graves 5/30/20

Hambone and Bimboface in the Alley (Act V, sc. 1)

(with apologies to The Bard, Prince Hamlet, and the country of Denmark)

[Hambone and Bimboface, two out of work musicians, wander down a lighted alleyway -- nothing better to do.

Spying something, Hambone reaches into a trashcan, pulls out and holds up an action-figure of "Bozohead", a famous comedian, now deceased.]:

Hambone: Whoa! Poor Bozohead.
I knew him, Bimboface
The guy was crackin' jokes all the time!
He was funnier than shit!
He used to call taxi's for me after the show when I was too drunk to drive home.

Ugh! This thing is gross! Geeez! Makes me wanna puke!

Man, look at the lips on that thing. I'd kiss 'em, I swear I would

Awww Bozohead, where're your wisecracks now? Huh? Your funny little drunken jigs? Your limericks?

You made me laugh so hard one time at dinner, that mashed potatoes came out of my nose. Remember?..."

-- Graves 11/13/12

Rising from the Fall from Height

You start in the "zone."

A place in which
making the wrong choice
the wrong move, seems
impossible.

Presented with a universe of possibilities
you infallibly - it seems -
pick the right color, the right
word, the right form, the right
turn of phrase; the creative energy fairly
coruscating in its transcendence.

Falling away from the zone
- from the height -
while recalling the view
is what finally drives artists mad.

To experience that potential of perfection
- because it's perhaps not
yet perceived as perfect
being ahead of its time -
that clarity of vision
that acuity of perception which
brings with it the assessment that
you just Know
what should come next.
Which note, theme or phrase
most precisely conveys
the message that you want
to create.

To be enticed by the Muse
to follow the precise path which
most directly – though often not
most immediately –
leads to the brilliance of creation and
the ability to balance on the razor's
edge of beauty, with no possibility
of a misstep.

To experience that divine madness which
in fact is the true height
of sanity, from which
everything

else – insignificant in
perspective - lies below
or beyond.

And to fall from this height while
retaining the memory of the view

is what drives artists to the point
of despondent madness.

A madness often too soon accepted
as permanent; absent the
realization that

in order to regain the height
one must simply rescale it.
One step at a time.

It is there and attainable, but only
for those with the determination
to reach it, and the will
to continue climbing.
You can do this, simply

because you decide to.
Or fail – simply, because you have not.

-Graves 10/5/22

Steel Flower/Concrete Soil

Thriving in the cold
neon light. She stands, reaching
hard for glittering stars
bent on making room in the sky.

Beyond the reach of divine intervention
bending shadows into fevered invention.
No turning back, no turning.
Shining fragility, calling
down the moon
down the moon
down the moonlight, in sheets, shining
in the darkness.

Hard like daylight.
Missing nothing.
Cold like ice. Steel flower
in concrete soil.
Eyes of sharpened steel, cleaving
away all excess until only
innocence remains.
Hard as diamonds -- no compromise.
Shining fragility, calling
down the moon
down the moon
down the moonlight, in sheets
shining in the night.

Drinking-in electricity
Straining beneath the weight of dreams.
The scar betrays nothing.
The holy glow tells all.
Terrifying in clarity.
Unbreakable simplicity.
Steel flower in concrete soil.
Beyond influence, beyond
redemption. Beyond weakness.
Shining fragility, calling
down the moon
down the moon
down the moonlight, in sheets
shining brightly in the night.

Delicate petals - vapor thin - razor sharp.
Cutting or striking brilliant sparks.
Mishandle her, and you will bleed.
Shining fragility, calling
down the moon
down the moon
down the moonlight, in sheets
Shining bright hunger
consuming the night.

                --Graves 3/11/17

"The Blonde"

Paint the sunset with me
in chords as vibrant as
burning clouds, shimmering in the air
mirroring the colors
of the setting sun.
Your music breathing holy life
into my naked words.

My words, which remain earthbound
without your wings
to soar them into ringing thunder.
Into sweet-voiced love.
Into pounding, reasoned attack.
Into stories, harmonized
with emotion in
rhapsodically simple
tunes, that make
the dirt
weep with joy.

You were the vessel
upon which my spirit soared
in youth.
The source of music
in my life.

And you
will be
again.

Your beautiful, golden back.
Your curves, that fit my arms
so well.
Your smooth, golden neck.
Your sensuous lower bout.

You and I have mesmerized
massive crowds;
brought tears to eyes, in
faces of stone.

Brought joy to those for whom
the hope of joy was past.
And won the hearts
of girls from
Acapulco to New Jersey.

My Blonde.
My loom of memories, yet
to happen.
My glass to see
the future refracted
through the past.

Your six voices
to my one.
Your song riding with me the winds
of change.

My fingers ache to
make you sing.
My calluses
with time have softened.
My voice has
changed in pitch.

You welcome, none the less,
whatever I bring.
And you sing.

Create the sky with me
and the lands.
Green-crested hills
and rushing water.
Outline the clouds with me
with your holy vibrant tones.

And bring me to another place at last.

     --Graves 10/8/17

Note: This piece is about my guitar, an acoustic six-string, which shimmers golden in the sunlight, because it is made of maple. A few decades ago, I had a three-hour set that I would perform in bars, and other places; basically, for anyone who would listen. For years, and to many people, my guitar was simply known as "The Blonde." (And for Tina, who for a long time was my other blonde - she just didn't know it.)

The Life of Dreams

Dreams don't die.
They just get dropped off somewhere, when
something else with more sparkle comes along.
Or when a soon-to-be former dreamer
decides that "real life" is more important.

REAL LIFE????

What the hell is more important than dreams!?!
"Real life" is a drafty bus stop in a rainstorm
in October, on a concrete sidewalk in a
bad part of town, compared to dreams!

You lose your dreams
and you might as well kill yourself right now.
(Or get some more dreams) because
your life is going to be pointless without them.

"Oh, but I have no more dreams... (*sob*)
they have all been taken from me by
a hard, hard life..."

"Dreaming's so difficult..."

whine

whine

whine.

Do you KNOW how hard it is to make new dreams?

It's the third easiest thing in the universe to do
after being alive; and looking (which is
the second easiest thing.)

If you want dreams, stop resisting them.
Make some!
It's not difficult.

And if you get tired of one
get rid of it and create a hundred more!

It's EASY! Unless for some reason, you've decided
that it's more fun to live in that damned bus stop
whining about how no one's provided you any dreams.
Waiting like some metaphysical socialist
for someone to give you the dreams
that they've taken from someone else, simply because
you're too wrapped around your own shortcomings
to come up with a few yourself.

Do you know how EASY it is
to come up with a new dream!?! Watch:

Think of something that you've always wanted to do.

Imagine yourself accomplishing it.

Imagine how that will feel
when you accomplish it.
Then, decide to do it.

Or not.

THAT'S ALL THERE IS TO IT!!!!!

Now, make a thousand more.
Or only three.
And if you get tired of one
or a hundred
get rid of it and make a hundred more!
No one's stopping you.
Except yourself!

"Dreaming's difficult . . ." Oh, please!

                --Graves 2/11/17

The Muse

She respects no schedule
save her own. And that
is the first thing one must learn
very, very well.

In her company
I have felt the light bending
through the cells of the inner veins of the crocus
unfolding slowly in sunlight and dew.

I have heard the moonlight singing
like a thousand haunted violins
as it slid coarsely across a thousand blades of frosted grass
in the winter night.

From her I have learned
that what appears to be
is more often than not:
not.

And that which is only imagined
has existed forever.

My wife has no concerns for where I go.
She knows that if she looks and cannot find me
I will be in the tent of the Muse.

      --Graves 10/21/15

The Perfect Life

It's brutal
but it's the perfect life.
Standing up there
on the stage.
Standing out there
in the light.
Taking hearts to destinations
that they've never seen.
Giving them flight.
Music on strings.
Words that sing.
You're giving them
all of them
each of them, wings.
It's brutal
but it's a perfect life.

–Graves 9/5/15

Poet's Note: I've been there. I'm not sure that I've ever written anything truer than this.

The Secret Handshake from God

Don't give me this
about writer's block!

Just start!
Start anywhere!
Just write!
There is ALWAYS more to write!
There is no shortage of pixels;
of paper
of blood for ink.
Just poke her! and you'll
wake the Muse.
Write! and she will respond to the calling. All
hot and trembling.

You see! You do! – LIFE
is the grist.
It's ALWAYS changing;
refracting differently.
Always a new angle.
Always a new angel.
Always a rift opening
in the pattern that
catches the eye
of the mind.

WRITE! Damn it! Paint! Compose! Sing!
What are you waiting on?
The mighty acknowledgment?
The secret handshake from God?

I think not . . .

                –Graves 8/11/12

This Afternoon the Muse Came to Visit

This afternoon, the Muse came to visit.

And now that She's left, there's a mess to clean up.
There's always a mess to clean up.
She didn't tell me that She was planning to show up.
She just arrived.
It seems like She always does this.
Damned inconsiderate.

I was planning to work on the yard.
Deadhead some roses.
Repair the fence.
Breathe a little.
And out of the blue, She just shows up and starts
handing out assignments.
"The point of view is off -- tighten the focus."
"The nuance is wrong, change the aspect"
"Too strong -- more subtlety."
"Too meandering – more concise."

You work
and you work
and work
and then She says:

"Do it a different way."

Inconsiderate, Annoying, Infuriating...
Damn it! I've got YARDWORK to do!

This afternoon the Muse came to visit.
And now that She's left, there's a mess to clean up.
But somewhere amongst the mess
she's left diamonds.

              --Graves 10/15/17

This Moment in Time

You determine this moment in time
no one else.
Its creation is yours.

You conceive it.
You shape it.
You give it life.

Yield the creation of this moment to another, and
you suspend yourself in air
above a chasm
hanging (or not) at their choice.
Your life no longer your own.

Fame, approval, permission granted
by another, may be
taken away.

Except by your own decision
what you create, cannot.

Yield your will to create
and your forward path becomes chosen
at the caprice of another.
The journey bereft of the
joyfulness born of creation.

You create your life
and include others (or not).
You create your future
and include others (or not).

Recall a time you were truly happy.
Wrapped in the arms of someone you loved.
Remember a time when you succeeded, and
things were joyfully real.
Remember a time that you won.

These things will be with you, always.
Regardless of what follows.

The creation of joy, of purpose
is within you. It is a gift that you give
yourself.

It is a gift that you share with others, or not.

Build your own life. Create your own dreams.
Live true to your own goals.
Speak your own truths.

None of these can be taken from you.
Unless you first elect it so.

                –Graves 2/18/17

Weaver (for Taylor Newton Stewart - Composer)

You weave, and the music swells.

Waves of textured sound, each
a thousand separate pieces of fractured glass
turn transcendently smooth in the woven
interaction.

Each note as clearly individual
as raindrops
falling through open sky.

Musical phrases join to form aural images:
Of the flight of a soaring bird;
the pain throbbing from an angel's harp;
broken glass on a dusty basement floor.
Of torrential rain in tumultuous air; swelling
to fill every
aspect of space.

I hear this in your music.

Melody, like the flight of a sparrow
carving a twisting, turning path, fast as lightning
through the cooling air of a huge barn
in the fading glow of an ebbing sun.

I hear the blade of grass pushing aside
dark loam in an empty field.
I hear the raging wind driving waves of sand
across the face of an ancient rock wall.

I hear the sound of time, bending
around a corner
in the dark.

I hear this in your music.

I hear chords made by clouds
drifting slowly in a rainy sky.

I hear musical notes falling in syncopation like
raindrops
cooling the thick, sultry night; merging
in swirling resolution as cleanly as
moonlight slicing
through dark

freezing air.

Poetry is carved
from ancient things.
It is chiseled from discarded pieces of time.
Images of what is, and what has
never been, moving with distinct direction.

Music is woven,
Fluidly crafted from that essence
which comprises universes. Vibrations
woven upon the loom of form.

Infinitely fine threads, balancing minute
variations, each determining the fate
of all the rest.

The fire you form, fuels the spirit of man.
It falls to you, the task of drawing music
from that which, left alone, are naught
but plain and simple sounds.
Yet when woven, ignite the fires of dreams.

I don't know how you do it.
I just listen.
     –Graves 9/15/17

Sequential glossary:

Musical phrase: A musical work is typically made up of a melody that consists of numerous consecutive musical phrases; each phrase having a complete musical sense of its own.

Syncopation: Syncopation is a general term for an interruption or disturbance in the regular flow of rhythm in a musical or other piece. It is used in many musical styles. It is used in many ways, but in the form of a back-beat, syncopation is used in virtually all contemporary popular music.

When I Go Among People

When I go among people
my quill sits in ink too long
and it gets soft. Too long
and there is too much to write.
Too long, and I have to cut a new point.

But then, things become
crisp.

When I go among people
scenes start to reel and
unravel in my mind. Plots
merge with counterplots
Points become subplots.
Characters shift and become
others.
The scene muddies
loses focus.

But sometimes the shift in POV
opens a door.

When I go among people
my colors run together.
They bleed past borders.
Complements become overly familiar and
start to dissonate --
turn to muddy puddles.

But sometimes, they become
a sunrise.

                          -Graves 1/9/10

Definition: POV: (*Screenwriting*) Point of View: That point from which the camera (and the audience) views the scene.

DEATH AND LIFE

Mortality

Basically, I don't believe in mortality.
Not in the long run.
There are times, though
that make you wonder.

In the long night, kidneys shutting down.
Shivering for hours because
you can't
get warm enough
in that hospital bed.
Mind too active to sleep.
Wondering if you'll see
the other side of two weeks, and
if so
what will it be like?

At some point you realize that
despite the skills of others
it __all__ depends on you.
Stay or leave. It's like a casual,
electrifying chat with God;
that the decision to ascend or
fall is yours.
Your choice.

Neither path is inherently wrong;
but the choice is yours alone, and
determines what you
will face, and how.

Keep or toss.
It's a life.
There will be others.

Yet
leaving is that leap
– that departure from
the familiar, pungently laced with
a sense of impending loneliness
and the uncertainty of
having to start over.
Even for those
who know the path.

The decision is yours.
The apprehension comes
in then resisting the decision that
you've made.

When the time comes
go with it. Decide. Rise – or leave.
And then do that with the confidence
of winning in that which you've decided.

-Graves 6/25/22

Poet's note: Mortality: "The condition of being mortal, or subject to death."

The point that confuses some people is that they don't differentiate between spiritual and physical mortality. They harbor a misconception that when the physical light goes out "that's all she wrote." It's an inaccurate assumption, as borne out by both history and science. Look around enough and you'll find this to be the case. In the meantime, I wish you well.

Apparency

The tired heart finally sleeps.
The laboring breath stills.
The warm eyes glaze.
And we grieve. The depth of our love
portending the depth
of that gut-wrenching grief, which claws pieces
from the beating heart, shatters life
and changes it forever.

The body fades.
The spirit endures.
Like it or not.

And depth of love, once again
defines the strength of connection.

After the loss, they remain for a time
and grieve beside us, though we
believe them gone: Bound up
as we are, in "seeing is believing."

Perception, though, extends beyond sight.
And sensing their sadness
we sometimes mistake it
for our own.

Belief, however, does not define truth.
Knowing defines truth.
The spirit, it seems, is not necessarily
subject to limits set by pronouncement.

Speak to them and they will hear.
Speak enough, and understanding occurs.
And things change.

I've had these conversations
more than once.
And I have seen things change.

Don't be shocked when you find
that your worst fear
your most mysterious adventure
your most binding chain; turns out not
to be completely as portrayed.

The future does not end
at death.

                –Graves 12/2/16

Farewell on a winter night – I will return
(a villanelle*)

My clock is ticking, tightly wound, behind its placid dial.
It walks where once it ran, and speaks of things I've left undone.
And though it makes you sad, I'm only leaving for a while.

The night is dark, and in its depth, appearances beguile,
yet darkness, though it hides the view, will bring the rising sun.
My clock, is ticking, tightly wound behind its placid dial.

Your reddened eyes show disbelief, and joy has left your smile;
Yet each of us will bid farewell once earthly course is run.
And though it makes you sad, I'm only leaving for a while.

So much is left to do, I've yet to span so many miles,
it seems unfair that I should leave what seems has just begun.
My clock, is ticking, tightly wound behind its placid dial.

I'll see you once again, my love, no virtue's in denial
of what we know we've done before and then again, begun.
And though it makes you sad, I'm only leaving for a while.

Persephone will still bless dew-kissed springtime with her smile;
while blinding fools to wonders clearly far beyond their ken.
My clock's still ticking, tightly wound behind its placid dial.
And though it makes you sad, I'm only leaving for a while.

--Graves 3/29/14

*POET'S NOTE: The villanelle is a poetic form consisting of five stanzas of three lines each (tercets) followed by a single stanza of four lines (a quatrain) for a total of nineteen lines which follow a strict pattern of rhyme and refrain. The first line of the first stanza serves as the last line of the second and fourth stanzas, and the third line of the sixth stanza. The third line of the first stanza serves as the last line of the third, fifth and sixth stanzas. It is an example of fixed-verse form; as opposed to free verse which is what I normally write.

Examples of the villanelle are Dylan Thomas' piece: *"Do not go gentle into that good night"*; and *"Mad Girl's Love Song"* by Sylvia Plath.

An Epitaph to Missing Friends . . .

In the cold, late darkness
last night
among the giant redwood trees; I heard
(what sounded, to my mind)
like a raccoon crooning
beneath a half-dark moon.

A sound as softly
sad as farewell, at the end
of the Earth.
And then it stopped . . .

I watched them grow from tiny things
smaller than a cat.
Five kittens batting
at the air with tiny hands
at imaginary foes.
Fighting tiny battles.
Rolling on their backs and
chasing each other, in
the exuberant playfulness gifted only
to the very young.

Five of them and their mother
eating peanuts that I had tossed
on the deck, behind
my house.
to get them to stay
for a while.

I wondered what you five would be like
after a winters growth.
How your tiny, masked
faces would change.
Wondered what you would become and how
your personalities would
evolve.
Looking forward to watching you
playing in the warm summer night. Tag
out on the deck, among
the peanuts and the plants.

This morning on the asphalt road I saw,
three tiny bodies, and suddenly I knew
the source of what I'd heard.
A mother crying in the night.
Whether they were on the way
to or from
my house for food – who knows?

Killed in a flash, by a driver too
careless to watch the road.
Three babies.
My friends.
Three tiny lights.
Snuffed out in a roaring flash.

I can hear the driver thinking
"Three raccoons. No one will miss you."

I will miss you.

                        -Graves 3/26/18

This piece was originally written in 2013

Waiting for You

The flow of time is soft
and silent.

It permeates and
moves. And
does not
stop.

Our sun
at last
softly set
once again.

The spaces between us
filled with darkness.
Until I could no longer
see.

I held your face in my hands. While
the cold night moved
between us, and jealous
in its absence of light
stole yours.

My lungs filled to their brim
with pain
and I sat
alone, watching you. Imagining
your chest moving
with the breath
that never came.

Finally, my lungs emptied
of sound.

Earlier that morning, I had wet a cloth and
carefully cleaned your face.
Not because I had to
but because I
still could.

You spoke to me then
in whispers
of flowers
and of the coming
spring, which
would brighten the woods

and promised

we would again walk the hills
and name the small birds
by their song.

I know that in quiet times
we spoke of the fact that
there is no one living
who has not met another
that they are

certain

they have known
before.

Not a single soul.

But this leap - despite
the number of times I know
that I've lept -
always
seems to be
one of faith.

You and I have danced
this dance
before.
So many times.
From its joyous resume
to its painful end.

This, to me
is as real as the daffodil
in my hand.

I sit now alone, and
wait. Remembering that
it is only
time.

I am waiting for our next walk
in the clean spring air.

The small birds
are waiting.

                –Graves 10/5/12

Funeral for a Friend

I don't do funerals.
They're after-the-fact affairs
too often filled with
broken pieces -- scattered shards.
Gaping wounds which
for the moment are not even
trying to heal. Everyone
looking backwards at
something that cannot be fixed;
when their view should be ahead. Not
to forget memories; but
to carry them forward.

But you were my friend.
You stood beside me, when
everyone else turned away.
And together we faced the world.
I don't do funerals
but I'd do yours.

–Graves 4/5/19

HUMOR

"And why," she asked haughtily, "should I say 'You bastards' instead of 'You sons of bitches?'"

On the Use of the Phrase "You Bastards!"

"Sons of bitches" seems so imprecise;
neither biting, impactful, it's just not concise.
When delivering a blow
you just want to know
the recipient's paid some kind of price!

"Sons of bitches" just sounds way too passive.
Not direct, kind of prissy and surely not massive
enough to connect with,
convey disrespect with
and frankly it's just not harassive.

"You Bastards!" is nicely contusive
Concise, clearly said and abusive
enough to impinge,
to make the guy cringe
and its meaning is never elusive.

"You Bastards!" is short, but more elegant
and actually really quite eloquent.
It's nicely concise.
poetically precise
And it always fits right in its element.

"You Bastards!" gives more satisfaction.
It really hits home with impaction.
It's never mistaken,
or leaves them unshaken
And generally causes some action.

"You Bastards!" is sonorously rich,
(and in plural it just fits the niche.)
For singular, though,
the best way to go
is cut loose with "You son of a bitch!"

See?

      -Graves 3/29/09

Nose Pickers

I saw you pickin' your nose today.
By God, I didn't know what to say.
It shocked me though to see you there,
just finger-busy and unaware
that your reputation as cool and complete
was going down to dull defeat.

I'm frankly shocked and taken aback;
that you'd even think of taking a whack
at sticking your finger in your nose
and workin' it 'til the dermis glows.
I never dreamed you were the kind
who used your fingers to unwind.

It's widely known, I'm sure you're aware,
about nose pickers everywhere;
they're actually a far cruder bunch
than you'd ever want to ask to lunch.
Largely because, (for at least one in ten)
you don't know where that finger's been.

Nose pickers're all underachievers,
indolent bums and basket weavers;
creatures of the worst possible kind.
Why, nose-picking can even make you go blind!
It's distracting in the worst possible way
and once you start, it won't go away.

I've heard that if the habit lingers
it'll make hair grow on your fingers!
Something else that gives me fits, is
frequent nose picking gives you zits!
Others will tell you (and this is tough)
that nose picking leads to harder stuff!

It worried me so much, I felt
like I'd been hit below the belt.
So I found the wisest man I could;
someone who absolutely would
give me advice so sound and true
that I would then know what to do.

I climbed tall mountains, searched the woods
I looked in places no one else could.
And finally upon the highest peak
I found a man with whom I could speak.
I found the wisest of holy men
someone on whom I could really depend.

And I asked him "Holy, reliable sir,
is it just me or do you concur,
that nose pickers should be roundly condemned;
the practice prohibited, forcefully stemmed.
And those who practice it, absolutely
shunned for living so dissolutely?

He looked at me and scratched his head,
he cocked his eyebrow, swallowed his bread;
then he answered me in a solemn voice
with a certainty that left no choice.
"Let him decide to cast the first stone
who's always left his nose alone."

                --Graves 4/27/12

Nipples

I've got 'em, you've got 'em.
On some people you can even spot 'em.
Some are dark, some are light
some of 'em only come out at night.

Some stand up and like to poke.
They star in seventh and eighth grade jokes.
Some are inverted and like to hide
but they're still loved both far and wide.

Babies like 'em, others too.
We have 'em in common, me and you.
Some are big, like silver dollars
some are little, tiny fellers.

Some are round, and cute as a button.
Some are oval, and artsy lookin'.
Some stand up, some are relaxed
some you won't see, so don't even ask.

Some are big, some are small
some you can barely see at all.
Some are pink, some are brown
some are even upside down.

Mine're about medium in size, I guess
and in the overall assessment
whatever size and whatever shape,
color or texture, asleep or awake;

they're perfect in whatever design
and frankly, I'm sorta partial to mine.
I'm pretty sure you like yours, too,
so the ones we've got will just have to do.

Amazingly, as common they are,
you can raise an eyebrow near or far;
just how much, is easily discovered,
just leave even one of them uncovered!

                -Graves 9/25/20

Deja Poo

"Oh Man!!!"
(lifting foot)
"Not again!?!"

                --Graves 10/15/10

On Doing

If you've decided you would
and you haven't, you should.
Unless you've decided you shouldn't
then don't.

If you haven't decided
then you should know
that the longer you don't
the more likely you won't.

If you've decided you would
and you haven't, you should.
Unless you've decided you shouldn't
then don't.

--Graves 9/1/17

On 'Maybes'

If you haven't decided you shouldn't
you should know that the longer you don't
the more difficult it will be to do.

If you've decided you would, and you haven't
you should.
Unless you've decided you shouldn't
then don't.

                     --Graves 3/3/16

Roots

I haven't shaved in four days.
And this morning, I can feel
the hair flowing
very
very
slowly
out of
my
face.

Like roots. Feeding
from the air.

I feel like a plant, turned upside down.
Walking on my branches, while
my roots seek nourishment
from the sun
and the breezes.

It's not an altogether inconvenient
arrangement.
When I walk in the rain without a hat
it's easier to water my roots.

     --Graves 3/3/16

The Church of Tits and Ass

The morning sun awakened me,
a chill was in the air.
The sound was loud from down the street,
there were people everywhere.

"What's all this racket going on?"
I asked as a man ran past,
"Everyone's going somewhere, and
I don't want to get there last."

He turned his head and said to me
"You're late, so hit the gas;
everybody's goin' down
to the Church of Tits and Ass."

St. Joe's a politician,
he comes from my state, back home.
A first class proselytizer,
he spouts verses from the tome.

He'll promise to grant your every wish
even get you resurrected.
He'll say anything you want to hear
to get himself elected.

You'll find him on any Sunday, preaching
filling the air with gas.
Belting out the holy writ
at the Church of Tits and Ass.

Mary is an anchor, on
the mainstream evening news;
spouting nasty, little stories
(her producer's personal views.)

She'll say whatever she's told to say
as long as she gets paid.
She'll do whatever she has to do
to get you to drink her kool-aid.

"Anything can be the truth
if there're decent ratings in it.
More viewers mean more commercial dollars
any way you spin it."

A sensational story's better
and she'll pretend that it's got class.
She's singing from the hymnal
at the Church of Tits and Ass.

Eloise the actress struts
in silky gowns so fine.
She'll play any part she's paid to play.
She'll parrot any line.

Her opinions are mostly blather
but she doesn't seem to care.
She'll shout them from the rooftops.
She's completely unaware

of the rolling eyes and shaking heads
every time she gives an opinion.
She's surrounded by her sycophants
and many cowardly minions.

No one's telling her differently
and she thinks that she's got class.
She's just been granted sainthood
in The Church of Tits and Ass.

Bernie, he's a public boy
his persona simply glows.
He rides his jet plane to and fro
as his reputation grows.

He's selling his predictions
calls them prophesies from God.
None of them come true, but
no one seems to think it's odd.

His followers are happy clams
waiting for wads of cash.
Taking it from the offering plates
at the Church of Tits and Ass.

Sandy's a pretty newbie
followed blindly by her squad
She wants everyone to sing her tune
to worship where she's trod.

She'd fancy herself the mother of God
but she thinks it'd be a demotion.
After all who else but she can walk
her way across the ocean?

She's busily trying to write her way
into the subject of every mass.
She's trying to steal the pulpit
at the Church of Tits and Ass.

I took a look around and saw
the shit was pretty deep.
The people there were silent, and
they looked a lot like sheep.

An usher pointed to a seat and
pushed me toward a pew.
"Just take a look around," he said,
"there's something here for you."

"If this is all you've got for me," I said,
I think I'll pass"
I've got far better places to be
than the Church of Tits and Ass.

      --Graves 1/8/21

A note on the poem:"The Church of Tits and Ass"

This is a satirical piece about integrity. It's about people who use pretense to achieve their ends, and those others whose sound-bite mentality allows them to get away with it.

If you saw the humor in this piece, then good for you. You haven't been sucked in. If, on the other hand, you found this piece in any way offensive or improper, then you may already be deeper in the mire than you should be.

--MG

The End of the World (with slight apologies to John Lennon for playing off of his piece: "Give Peace a Chance.")

Ev'rybody's talkin 'bout Nos-tra-DA-mus
Nos-tra-DA-mus
Nos-tra-DA-mus

Ev'rybody's talkin 'bout Re-vel-A-tion
Re-vel-A-tion
Re-vel-A-tion

Ev'rybody's talkin 'bout the MAY-an CAL-endar
MAY-an CAL-endar
MAY-an CAL-endar

All -- they are say--ing is
it's the end of the world.

All -- they are say--ing is
it's the end of the world.

Yawn

Sounds scary
until you realize that Nostradamus was
a French poet who wrote in ambiguous quatrains
of dubious interpretation like
any cagey carny fortune teller.
Great drama for the bored.

And Revelation (prior to being heavily, heavily
edited)
was written by a hermit
hoping for the fall of Rome in
a violent sea of molten lava.
It's a little outdated.

And the Mayan Calendar was based
on the 5126-year Long Count calendar
which (BTW) starts over again this year.
(Much like my need to buy a new appointment book.)
It's been a little misinterpreted.

So far, I've survived at least twenty
Sure-fire.
Honest to God.
Absolutely authentic.
Money back, guaranteed.
End of the world prophecies.
Including the Cold War -- which was more of a day-
to-day
thing.

Someone made money off of
each
one
of them.

So, I'm sure that you'll pardon me
if I make my New Year's Eve, 2013 reservations
early
this year.
And pre-order my 2013
appointment book.

                --Graves 12/19/12

NOTE: The story behind this piece is that the Mayan Calendar officially ran out of dates on December 21, 2012. This led many people to believe that the Mayans had predicted the end of the world on that date. Personally, it made more sense to me that – after projecting their calendar a few thousand years into the future -- the guy who put it together, looked at it and said something like: "Good enough! I'm sure that someone else in the next few thousand years with some time on their hands will probably be happy to add a few thousand more years."

IMMORTALITY

A Movement in the Air

Your future follows your choice.
Who you were
what you've done
what you've failed to do; mattered once.
Not now.

Your self-doubt
your second-guessing is baggage
that someone left behind to
clutter your life
in hopes that you might, at some future point
stumble over it in a darkened hallway, and upon
regaining your feet
choose a path not your own.

Decide that your future is that of a hero
and it shall be.
Decide to allow yourself to fail
and that fate is yours.

You need no spells to grant permission
nor talismans. No contrivances of old.
You are permission.

You've always known that this is true.
You've felt it stirring
in your soul. A quiet disturbance.
An awareness in the back of your mind
like a movement in the air. Incessant
like the transit of the moon.

Your future is as you decide.

                –Graves 4/2/16

Stardust

We are the creators of infinite dreams.
Each of us.

Yet many work so very hard
to attain that hollow acclaim
which comes with being
little more than meat.

A hamburger.
Wrapped in a GMO-laced bun
with mustard and onions.
And maybe some fries.

The holy end-game, little more
than the accumulation of trinkets. And
the universal in-and-out.

Which (in the scheme of things) is
no more than an entertaining pinball machine
plugged into a wall, sitting in a corner
at one end of a vast realm of Magic.
A vast realm of Magic.

The stars are dust compared to us
they shine in the void of space.
Bright lights in the sky, creating nothing.

We are the creators of infinite dreams.
Gods wrapped in delusion.
Shuttered by amnesia.
Made idiots by distraction with baubles;
tiny, twinkling, glittering baubles.
Mumbling confusedly in a darkened room.
Playing inconsequential games
with broken fingers.

The only thing;
the only acceptable resolution to this
is to turn the tide.

We are the creators of infinite dreams.
Each of us.
We are so much more than stardust.

                     –Graves 1/23/17

The Dance

We are
each of us
an individual viewpoint
of creation.

We are
each of us
a Creator-in-disguise.
On vacation from the "big job."

We are dancers
of the eternal pavane. Indulging

in a casual pirouette
to spin
a galaxy on its way. Or
a playful
tour en l'aire
to remind the planets how it's done.

Working out
the choreography of a
freestyle jazz routine
on the head
of a pin;
with the rest of the angels.

We dance.

We weep.

We sow joy.

We inspire.

We dance: Trailing songs

and the poetry of a million lives lived.

>   –Graves 12/14/12

Glossary:

Pavane: A stately court dance by couples that was introduced from southern Europe into England in the 16th century.

Pirouette: A full turn of the body on the point of the toe or the ball of the foot in ballet

Tour en l'aire: (French: "turn in the air"), in ballet, a complete single, double, or triple turn in the air.

Tightrope

Life is a tightrope strung between two deaths.
The one behind
and the one ahead.

Your decision determines the height
of the wire that you walk.
Nothing else does.

Some lines are tied so near to the ground, that they
sag wearily against the earth.
These are very, very safe ropes to walk.
Heartbreakingly tepid.
No entertainment-value.

Others are rigid, high wires that tremble and sing
in the wind.
Wires set so high in the air, that
huge, white clouds roll slowly by
beneath them.

And upon these wires, walk heroes.
Not because of the height of the wire
but because they are heroes.

Entire lives are played-out
on wires in the air.
You'd think that this familiarity
would breed fluidity, and
a certain contempt for falling. Yet, so many
are so very careful
to cautiously place
one foot
in front
of the
other;

fearful that a single misstep, might be fatal.

And the way I see it, that's the problem.

The worth of walking the wire
is in the view that's only seen
when you are no longer transfixed
by the sight of the ground
far, far beneath your feet.

The real trick, is to learn
how to walk between clouds
without needing the rope.

     --Graves 3/4/16

Connecting Dots

We live engulfed
by the lower part of the same sky.
All of us.

We breathe pieces of air
which we have shared by proxy
(from time to time)
on a warm Spring day, when the sky held

just

so

many clouds.

We see the crimson afterglow which heralds night
and speaks of things to come. And wonder
what the day has left in store.

We love.

We hold sleeping dreams, until it is time
for them to wake or
to be set free.

We sleep.

We waken – for sleeping can only go on so long
and move (in one fashion or another)
through the day.

We hunger for that which we do not have
(yearn seems such an affected, small word
in this case)
if only in noting its absence.

We relish that which we realize we have. And lose
at some point, that which we do not.

Lines between dots connect us all.
Connect us all.

We die.
We wonder about what comes next.

–Graves 1/1/15

Notes: In activity books for children there are often pictures which are formed by connecting the dots with a line. Connecting the dots forms the picture. As humans, we have many dots in common. The pictures are very similar, but too often the dots remain unconnected. The commonalities unappreciated.

Actors (Death as a Masquerade)

We are: All of us
actors upon the spherical stage.

Actors who have agreed
to remember to forget
that we are more
than a single note in
symphonic resonance.
More than a single blink
in the vista of time.

We have agreed to not know
why the play takes place.
So that we may feel, each time
its surging, sparkling joy as though
it were a thing experienced
for the first time.

We have agreed to wear
the costume and to ring
the curtain down. Applause or not.
Curtain call
or not. Because playing
is all.

And so we play.
Spinning the shimmering web of creation.
All of us.
Some of us just remember
to forget, better than others.

~~~~~~~~~~~~~~~~~~~~–Graves 2/8/20

Notes:

"Ring the curtain down": (theatrical idiom) To lower a theater curtain, usually at the end of a play.

Curtain call: A curtain call occurs at the end of a performance when the actors return to the stage to be recognized by the audience for their performance. In a musical performance that went particularly well, it usually involves the performance of an additional song in response to the enthusiastic applause of the audience.

Hide and Seek

Death is now an old friend, waiting
to share rich, black coffee.

The Day finally slides softly away.
The warm, starless night fills my eyes
like honey from a broken jar.
My grip betrays me, falls away.
And my fierce fight to hold you forever, fails.

The wind blows. The loose red dirt stirs.
The Earth moves through the night sky.

Time weaves dark ribbons deep
through memories, cutting out light.
An absence on the edge of recollection; you
keep me from rest. A vague, haunted presence
you wake me from sleep.

The purpose of the universe is:
A place to play a long (a very long) game.
Sometimes we remember this in dreams.
Playing, but never letting ourselves know.
For knowing would ruin the game.

The reward of playing hide and seek
as we do -- you and I - is the delight in "once again."

Time ticks past in lifetimes. And then
a rich, familiar cadence. Perhaps a melodic note
in a voice. The casual turn of a once-forgotten, yet
suddenly familiar phrase, from a time long past.
A personality that kindles mine too intensely, to be
chance.

There is no mistaking this.
This is not just chance encounter.

     --Graves 4/3/18

The Artery (Times Square)

Flash-frozen pulse
of a million cells. Destiny
flowing in kaleidoscopic
direction. Focused
for now by the traffic-light
pump of an urban heart.
Dreams burning bright, rushing
into the future.
A million untold stories
passing by.

                    --Graves 1/22/19

Travelers

We travel eternity, balanced
nimbly on now.

On the tip
of the fulcrum that
lies in-between past and future.
Riding it like some
temporal surfboard: immobile, while
everything else races past.

Travelers. The choice always, between paths.

Decision always, the point of pivot
between convergences/divergences.
Possibilities.
Currents in the stream.
Echoes in a dark room.
Offshoots on the map.
Routes across the ice.

Time is not a line. It is a
plane of possibility.
Everywhere is now
once you arrive. And
gone when you leave.

We all travel our own threads
which together, weave the
forming fabric of now.
Your fate
lies anywhere you choose, amongst
the convergences/divergences.

Traveling through time is not unlike
stepping to the left
just different.
It seems difficult to do
because we're already doing it.

      --Graves 7/19/23

Truth and Death

There is death
and there is the truth. And
as with other things
sometimes what seems to be the case
is not.

Spirit appends to meat.
A juxtaposition of metaphysical opposites.
The story is that we are only
a clever package of
bones, muscle and skin
of eyelashes and sensation; carrying
a soul in a satchel (as it were).
And as such, we live only one life.

But there is you – and there is it.
There is you – and there is this meat-thing.

Bodies die all the time.
You cannot. Not once
in all of the seeming eternity of
your existence; have you died.
This might be difficult to recall
just now, sitting there reading poetry.
But it is true.

For some, this is a light too bright to see.
It hurts their eyes. Too much truth.
And they turn away; selecting death
as their guiding reality. Delighting
in the grim drama. Believing that this
is all there is. Meat and death.

Beyond this place though, is not death.
For some, however,
(bereft of the bigger picture)
it is in some way entertaining to
think that this is so.

Beyond this place is
continuation.
For that is what's next.
If you want to think of it as next.

Those who tell you otherwise
are simply striving to bend you
to their servitude. To bind you
using the liability of believing
that you are mortal. For them
control is made easier using
fear of death as the lash
that drives you.

There is death.
And there is truth.

Your journey never ends.   --Graves 9/11/19

LIFE

The View from the Lighthouse

I have seen the storms
far-off and approaching.
I have watched the crashing waves
yet to come
run their course.
I have heard the howling wind
in the dark wet night.

I have watched the tides.

I see the rocks that lie in wait
beneath the shiny surface
of the calm sea.
I see the slow
unstoppable
swell
of the tsunami
seeking
to subsume
the shoreline.

The sea itself is made of changes. Always
changes.

Some sudden and violent.
Some transient and fleeting.
Some deadly and permanent.

With perspective
you learn the difference.

Vicissitudes can kill you.
Even the word sounds like
choppy water.

Life can turn on a dime.
Let it.
Allow it to turn, and then
ride it
in your direction.

Anything else, and you founder
or become at last becalmed.

With perspective
you learn the difference.

Just because the water is choppy
does not mean
disaster is certain.
Adrift is not death.
It is simply

adrift.

Know the stable point of land.
Know the star that does not fail.
Know very well, the decision
that means more to you
than life.

And on that, plot your course.
And never

waver.

Do not panic
when the wind hits a fresh gale
when the waters turn angry
and the masts begin to creak and strain.
That is simply the way
of the sea.

Sailing is at its most exhilarating
when the sails are full
and pulses pound. Provided
you stay the course
and ride out the storm.

Don't change direction, based
on a single stretch of
heavy weather.
If what you seek
was near at hand
you would not be sailing.

 —Graves 8/26/11

The Mode of the Hummingbird

When you drop it
a stone falls.
It happens.
Your opinion on the matter is not required.

When you blame
your shortcomings on another, you
swear blind fealty to a lie.
You abdicate the dream.
You hand the knife
to the highwayman and lay bare
your throat.
Because this attitude will eventually kill you.

It's harsh.
But it's true.
Like a falling stone.

Those who seek to blind you, or
bend you to their will
will tell you otherwise. It is
their benefit that interests them. Not truth.
If you bend, you become
their marionette.
Jeanne d'Arc can cite you
chapter and verse on this.

At the beginning, nothing
is determined.
Your road does not begin
at its end.
It does not start in a state
of completion.
It leads not yet to failure
nor to success.
That which you seek to achieve
is there before you.
Waiting.

The hummingbird does not see himself
as small.
He simply sees the world
as large.
And in that mode
he flies.

The limit placed on you
by another
is a lie.
The limit that you place
on yourself
is your chain. It is
the barrier you cannot
surmount.

Unless (of course) you change
your mind.

And when you truly, fully
change your mind
you will find that removing the barrier
is very much like
taking off a coat on a hot day.

After all

the world is
only large.

–Graves 12/9/14

Glossary:

mode n. 1. a. A manner, way, or method of doing or acting.

Jeanne d'Arc: (Eng. Joan of Arc) (ca. 1412 – May 30, 1431) was born to a peasant family in northeast France. She said that she had received visions from God instructing her to support Charles VII and recover France from English domination late in the Hundred Years' War.

She was sent by the uncrowned King Charles VII to the siege of Orléans as part of a relief mission; and gained prominence after the siege was lifted in only nine days. Several additional swift victories led to Charles VII's coronation at Reims.

On May 23, 1430 Jeanne was captured at Compiegne by the English-allied Burgundian faction. Subsequently, she was put on trial by the pro-English Bishop of Beauvais, Pierre Cauchon on a variety of spurious, politically-motivated charges in an attempt to undermine the legitimacy of the succession of King Charles VII. She was found guilty of heresy and burned at the stake. She was about 19 years old.

Twenty-five years after her execution, an inquisitorial court authorized by Pope Callixtus III examined the trial, pronounced her innocent and declared her a martyr.

The Life That You Create

Blame it on the time of day
blame it on your fate.
Blame it on your parentage
or that you were born too late.
The fact, when you come down to it's
not open to debate.
The only life you're going to get
is the one that you create!

>   --Graves 11/8/15

Runway 24, Lukla, Nepal
  (The Attainment of Dreams

To reach the summit of Everest
you must land on Runway 24
in Lukla, Nepal.

There is no other way.

It has a cliff at one end.
A mountainside at the other.
It is only
one thousand
five hundred
feet long.

It is the most dangerous runway
in the world.

But it is the gateway
to dreams.

To reach Everest
you must walk the Khumbu Glacier.
But first
you must scale the death trap that is the Khumbu
Icefall.

To earn the chance to do either
you must land on Runway 24.
You must commit.

Runway 24 is the step beyond common reality.
Every prior experience
is shared with those who are content
to live on ordinary ground.

The flight from Kathmandu takes 35 minutes.
The weather changes
quickly.

When the opportunity for flight presents itself
you must take it.
Or remain below.

You must commit.

There is no other way.

The light changes on the summit of Everest
from minute to minute.
No two climbers ever

see exactly the same view
from the height.

As sure as the clouds
of ice crystals rise
on the ragged winds
like a plume
from the summit of Everest

it is there
for the taking.

To attain
you must commit.
You must land on Runway 24.

        –Graves 10/2/15

NOTE: The Khumbu Icefall lies at the head of the Khumbu Glacier, on the Nepali slopes of Mount Everest, not far above Base Camp. The icefall is one of the most dangerous stages of the South Col route to Everest's summit. It is estimated that the glacier advances 3 to 4 feet down the mountain every day. Large crevasses open with little warning. The towers of ice found at the icefall have been known to collapse suddenly, sending huge blocks of ice tumbling down the glacier. They can range from the size of cars to the size of 12-story buildings.

This poem is dedicated to those who have landed.

6 Secrets: In the Key of Dali

One:

I
dropped
the Key.

And saw it

fall,

and vanish

into

sunshine splashing
on the celestial
hardwood floor, in

drops
of glowing
steel, burning holes
in the fabric
of dreams, and

dripping through
as cold rain;
sealing the ground
of the universe
underneath
the glowing sky, turning
the firmament below the
floating castles
into mud.

Two:

The busy sun -- always
looking,
looking,
looking
for yellow
gold to line his coffers --
who sees all
(except the night)

blinks

in envious realization
that the

only

winner is the empty
void, which
requires

nothing

from which to create
whatever it wishes
and spin it into
a crystalline reality
formed from
the clearest of,
truths -- unbreakable in
their simplicity.

Three:

The Infinite,
azure sky,
weeps with happiness
(for lack of a better excuse)
secure (for now)
in the knowledge

that space,
alone,
is
what prompts the transit
of universes.

That thing
which separates
giants from their
dreams --

is space

alone.

Four:

The Priestess,
and The Crown Prince of Espresso,
(lowly occupants of time
and the noisy
corridors of
gravity)

are madly
orchestrating
a charge against
the legions
of limp biscotti who weep
with shame; over
their lost integrity, spent
on a momentary
dunk
in the cup
of inconsequential depravity.

Five:

I was busy, reading
palms, for small change,
searching my crystal
map - for a
way
out of this elevator,
into an
alternate place of
pastoral bliss
and scented magnolia trees.

When I stumbled,

(alerting
the darkness
to the new light,
breaking
into scintillating shards
against the
morning sky)

waking watchdogs
of angels
listening like
razors,
waiting to
reveal
secrets without
bothering
to understand them. (Who knew?)

Six:

The true secret is: That

there are
no
secrets --

beyond our choice.

>   --Graves 6/24/10
>   (with thanks to Salvador Dali)

A Simple Step

If you want
to change the world,
then your path is simple.
All you must do.
is change
the world.

Nothing more.

                    --Graves 6/30/12

An Unwasted Life

Before you set about to do
anything
ask yourself "So what?"
"If I do this, what
will come of it? Is the result
something worth pursuing?"
Look through, to the
end of the endeavor.

If the reason for the pursuit
or its result
doesn't make sense to you
if it doesn't fill you with
the pride of accomplishment
or joy
don't do it.
There is no point.

Perhaps it's caprice. Perhaps a whim.
It will get you no closer to fulfillment
than you are right now
except that you will have
wasted the time that you have
in the pursuit of
something
of ephemeral value
at best.

Ask yourself "So what?"
Or you'll end up with
a life that's been frittered
away on amorphous inconsequential.

Once you discover that
thing that resonates
through to your soul
set your course, and on
that path strive for perfection.
Pursue that
dream and never let it go.
Its accomplishment will
bring you happiness.

     --Graves 10/12/22

Angel Rising

Despite all

I rise.
On golden wings
of my own creation.

I am the human spirit.
I am that which endures all
and survives!

I am that which turns
the page and continues
forward!

I am irrepressible.
You cannot stop me!

I am the human spirit.
I rise!

                –Graves 1/19/19

Barriers to Flight

Icarus could not fly.

Until he decided that he would.
So it was, with:

The Wrights, at Kittyhawk
who did what others had not.

And Charles
on fixed-wings, speeding
across the icy, dark Atlantic sky
under shining, white stars.

And Amelia
riding the whipping wind. Soaring
high above the wide
wide
blue Pacific.

And Neal, Buzz and Michael
in the silent, hot lunar dust.
All eyes fixed to the sky.

And the Others . . .

The barrier to flight, is the belief
that flight is impossible.

Believe strongly enough
and it will be.

"Impossible." Covers a multitude of sins.
For such is the abandonment of a dream.
And there are few, more damaging sins
than leaving dreams to die.

Heads have been beaten bloody against
brick walls for not realizing
that the wall
is not the real barrier.

Before Icarus decided to fly
he could not.

If you are thinking to yourself:

". . .and look what happened to Icarus."

That's why you can't.

$\qquad$ –Graves 3/4/16

Barriers

Between here and success
are barriers.

For them to make any difference
you first have to see them as barriers.
And then you have to believe
that they can stop you.

It's pretty simple.
And if you're accustomed to barriers stopping you
it can seem unavoidable, and
stupid to think otherwise.

All things outside of yourself
that seek to stop you
you can surmount.
If you decide to.

I have never told you anything
truer than this.

And if you don't believe
What I'm telling you now;
that's a great example of a barrier.

A barrier is an excuse to turn back.
It's an acceptable response to fear,
that you can buy-into without
looking bad to others, because:
"Well, it was just too difficult."

Sure.
Give up.
No one will think less of you.
"No one could have done it."

Of course, you could
have done it: If you'd gotten
brighter in your approach
tougher in your pursuit; or
if you'd refused to quit.

A barrier is a reason to remain
comfortably bound by the familiar.
It can also be an excuse
to avoid attainment.

For, to end the game by winning
is nevertheless to end the game.
And without the game, what's
left to do?

There's a difference
between a barrier
and the wrong path.
The wrong path was
wrong from the start.
The right path is
one in which you believe
and always have.
You know it's right
daunting or not.

"It's always darkest just before the dawn."

Astronomically, not true.
The saying comes more from
the observation of barriers. And
their relationship to
persistence and success. In truth, it's
actually darkest around 2:00am.

Barriers often appear to be
most insurmountable
just before they fall.
Ask anyone
who has achieved goals.
It's true.

To surmount barriers requires persistence, and
maybe a different approach.

A barrier is an odd form of entertainment.
It is the oldest form.
And the most basic:
You create barriers in order
to find out whether you can best them
and win, despite them. Because
if you just went out and won all the time
where's the fun in that?
It gets mind-numbingly boring after a while.

If you thought about barriers differently
you would ignore them and
just succeed.
Simple, really.
But, so is life.

–Graves 4/17/20

Back story: Somewhat ironically, the power in my house went out this morning (5/5/13 – the date of the first draft of this piece) at 9:00am; shortly after I started this piece. I completed it in the dark. Just thought you might find that amusing.

Beatitudes

Blessed are those who refuse to fail
For they shall attain
impossible heights.

Blessed is the child who rides out life
alone, and blooms despite all.
for his is the resilience
of the unstoppable.

Blessed are those who give advice
and do not require that it be followed;
for they will be called friends.

Blessed are those who care enough to change
conditions
where others will not.
For their lives, while perhaps more trying
will make the greatest difference.

Blessed are those who right the scales;
for their gift to the world
is sanity.

Blessed are those who follow Jerry Garcia and the
boys.
For they shall be called "Deadheads*"
Wait . . . what?

Blessed are those who acknowledge and forgive the past.
For they will have
the clearest view of the future.

Blessed are those who grace the world with
new viewpoints, new games, and new vistas.
For theirs is the crown of creation.
And they will be the suppliers of dreams.

Blessed are those willing to honestly help
without hidden agenda;
for they will ease the burden.

Blessed are the defenders and healers of souls;
for they guard the route to eternity.

Blessed are those who understand the power of responsibility
and the fruitlessness of revenge.
For theirs will be the sanest perspective.

Blessed are those who strive to travel beyond the edge of what is known.
For theirs is the uncharted realm.

Blessed are those who understand, and move forward
even under the most daunting conditions.
For they will forge the forward path.

And blessed are those who come back.
For some will call them angels.
And they will save
the world.

–Graves 1/28/11

Notes: *"Deadheads" is a term which was affectionately given to fans of the rock band "The Grateful Dead," which achieved iconic status in the 1970's. Jerry Garcia was the band's leader.

Brushwork

Blame another for your circumstances
and you paint yourself as
victim.

Every
single
brush stroke
is yours.

You mix the paint.
You choose the canvas.
You select the colors.
You paint the scene.
You do the brushwork.
Start living, and you are
the painter.

Paint the picture that you want.
Or not. But while you stand there with
dirty brushes, a smeared palette and
paint-stained hands; don't pretend
that someone else painted it.

Every color-choice was yours.
Every hue, every selection of technique
every stroke. Every decision to
paint – or not. Every space filled with
color – every space left as bare canvas.

Any moron can blame.

An artist creates.

You have more
power than you may realize.
Maybe you need to amp up your
courage to match it.

Decide to do it
or not.
It's on you.

Van Gogh's paintings were not shaped by critics.
Monet didn't buckle under
to the Academie des Beaux-Arts.
Martin Luther King didn't stop dreaming.
Dylan, Baez and the others wouldn't shut up.
Why should you?

                --Graves 7/30/22

Catch and Release

Freedom is a supple thing.
Slippery like a fish in water; sliding
among wet currents with
the ease of belonging.

The potential to set out
to create a chosen effect, and
to shape the space and future
created therewith, determines freedom.

You become captive when
you hold so fiercely to intent
that it becomes a thing wrapped in
loss and pain, if not achieved.

For in so becoming, it rules you
instead of the other way around.

When the desire to create a specific effect
is gripped too tightly – for too long;
the fingers atrophy and are not
able to painlessly let go and reach
for the next dream.

Bound then, to desperate effort
dreams become anchors.
Trammeled channels which
inhibiting other options
dominate a life otherwise happy
and filled with mutable paths.

Freedom is catch and release.
To exist, it must be catch and release.
And catch again.

    –Graves 11/6/19

Note: Catch and Release: The practice – in fishing – of catching a fish and then letting it go without killing it.

The Cutting Edge of the Blade

It's not a place where you live by bits.
It's bright and it's fast, and you live by your wits.
It's a place where the best part of life is played.
Out on the cutting edge of the blade.

No need to be nervous; no need to hide;
just hang on tight and enjoy the ride!
The game is big and broad and wide,
on the cutting edge of the blade.

You make it big or else you fade.
Life's like that, the price gets paid.
Out there is where the fortunes are made,
on the cutting edge of the blade.

Or, you can hide and resist all motion,
live with fear as your primary emotion.
But when you die, or you start to fade,
you'll wish that you'd lived on the edge of the blade.

It's always hotter and brighter, you see;
the light is clearer, the winds blow free.
You can see to the edge of eternity
from the cutting edge of the blade.

It's a place where dreams fly high and wide.
A place where you can enjoy the ride.
Life out there is magnified,
on the cutting edge of the blade.

The ideas are brilliant, the music is cookin'
the people are out there pushin' and pushin'.
They're looking to make a place of their own,
on the cutting edge of the blade.

When you wish upon a star
and wake up where the clouds are far
you'll realize just where you are:
On the cutting edge of the blade.

All these things I know are true.
Like I know that I'll be hearing you
laughing as you enjoy the view
from the cutting edge, of the blade.

--Graves 12/1/17

*Cutting edge -- slang, meaning:

1. Far in advance of what is considered ordinary, or day-to-day.
2. Exceptional, advanced, innovative.
3. Closest to the point of innovation.

Darkness and Light

First there is darkness.
Until there is light.

Light is not the natural way of things. It is
created. Absent light
the universe is dark.

There is first absence
until you approach.
I feel your warm breath on my neck.
Your presence (as it always does) changes
the essence of my experience. Much

in the way that there is
first cold. Until it is
replaced with heat.

There is inaction before action
status quo before change
stillness before motion.

Prior to and following hatred there is
the willingness to understand.

We attract that which we fear
because we work to push it away.
In pushing, we must make contact.
And in contacting, we draw it near.

Create, instead, in the direction in
which you would travel.
And the things you fear will
drop away behind you. They cannot
keep up without your help.

The reason that we do not achieve, has nothing
to do with anyone else.
Life is as we perceive it and
as we empower it. Prior
to perception, it is not our life.

     –Graves 9/17/21

Decision

The dream does not exist, which
has not in its conception, come
coupled with challenge
as its birth-twin.

Alike, no wish exists
that in its forming thought is void
of gauntlet thrown
to make it so.

Life concatenates
challenge to challenge.
That's what makes it
Life.

To wake and dress, or drink
hot coffee
without spilling.

To ascend
the vertical rock face
ice-covered
in a live, raging
gale. Or to fall

into hopeless
riotous love, never
to be the same. Ever.

Life concatenates
that is

what makes it
Life.

The path was void before you came
win or lose
you decide which fork to walk.
And you
alone.

Who refuses this, is soaked too deep
in need to blame, his head
too thickly bound in batting
to hear the holy
songs.

You
and you alone decide:
poison or
life.

The dream does not exist, which
has not in its conception come
coupled with challenge as its birth-twin.

Delight or
poison.
you decide.

      –Graves 12/24/10

Definition

It's not who you claim to be that counts.
The surface of the lake mirrors the sky.
An illusory claim to reality. Nothing more.
Pretense lacking depth.

Your actions define you.
Nothing else.

No transgression escapes without consequence.
And omission, though unfelt at first;
like a razor, cuts deepest.

The warm, willing love left behind.
The gift, selected with care, and
never delivered.
The act of kindness
delayed until too late.
The wrong; witnessed
and left unopposed.

The unwritten is never seen.
The unspoken, never heard.

Your actions form the poetry
or the cliche
that is your life.

Sonnet
Novel
Epithet
Graffiti.

Edit.

Or not.

It's your life.

          --Graves 9/19/21

Distraction

Here I sit
in the sunshine, among
the redwoods.
On the forest floor.
A soft bed of needles
a thousand years old
and contemplate massive trees
older than the country. Trees older
than the typeset word.

The majesty of golden
sunlight in the cool morning
sifting through the outstretched green
branches, making them
glow as it fights to get through.

I sit here among this majesty
and sometimes
all I can think of is
how good a ripe, sweet
peach would taste
right now. Its juice
running down my fingers.

Sometimes life is like that.

                      --Graves 4/2/22

Doorways

Every mind is a doorway, that
opens into a different
universe.

It may not be
radically different from yours
but it is different.

Each is a metaphysical space, as
high, as wide and as deep as
the universe that you perceive.

Each branches out
in directions that differ from yours.
Your own universe seems infinite.
So does each of theirs.

How many infinities of size
do you see
In a glance at passersby
on the street?

What wonders exist, in
each of those universes?
What terrors?
What loves? What dedication?
All of the aspects
(in greater or lesser degree)
that you own;
exist in each.

We are not simply human.
We are doorways to the infinite.

> – Graves 5/31/20

Dreams - (in four short acts)

Act I:

Your dreams are
your
path

from tragedy
to
joy.

You
decide
to walk the path
or not.

Staying home with
dying dreams
though warm and safe

is tragic.

Act II:

You have never dreamed that
which you cannot
achieve.

And you never will.

This fact
terrifies
some who dream

into disbelief.

It terrifies far more
those who fear

dreamers.

This truth is
as simple

and real

as dust motes
riding sunbeams.

Act III:

Fears:

You create them
permit them and
adopt them
You enshrine them
and worship them.

And that is the

only

reason
that they do not
leave.

It is only your fears
that will stop your dreams.

This has always been
a comfort
to the courageous

and to those who suddenly realize that
they are about
to become

courageous.

Act IV:

Joy is in
your right hand
tragedy
in your left.

Both are already in
your grasp

–Graves 4/30/10

Eight Couplets: A Reminder

Live in your thoughts, wrapped up in your dreams
and life will be nothing but: "What might have beens."

The fame that you seek isn't found in your head
and life isn't lived snuggled up in your bed.

Sleeping is pleasant, but never replete
with the red hot adventures that wait in the street.

Pretending is fine, make-believe can be cute
but posturing never will get you the loot.

So sharpen your ears and put this in your head
there's plenty of sleeping time after you're dead.

Life's full of wonder and lessons to teach
but you'll miss out on all if you're slow to your feet.

A boring existence is likely to pass
and it will, if you never get up off your ass!

                --Graves 6/5/20

Heroes (To Erin)

I grew up believing in heroes.
I still do.

There are heroes in each one of us.
I know this for a fact.
You may have to dig quite deep
to see that this is true.

And when you do, you'll
recall a time
when a hero's light
shone forth from you
brighter far than any sun.

Recall how you continued then
when others fell – and you prevailed.
Recall how you held truth above all else
when others fell to lies.
Recall the fight that fell to you
when no one else could see it through.
Recall the times you won.

And if – just now – it's hard for you
to scan the past and see these times
it's not because it never was.
Keep looking – you will find them.

And breathe again a hero's breath
and do those things a hero does.
For you were there when right prevailed.

Be there again.
It's a new day.

      --Graves 11/4/16

Inner Voice

Ignore your inner voice
that sound that brings you
joy and keeps you pure.
And you will die miserable
and old.

Listen, and remain true
to that calling. Dance
to its music with
abandon! And
death will never
catch you.

                    --Graves 4/11/22

Integrity

No one ever flew by
fleeing from the howling wind.
To fly, the wind must be embraced
and flown.
The difference between flight, and flight
is vast.

No one ever grew by
being broken to a mold.
Growth requires an unencumbered path
from darkness to the light.
The difference between a lesson and illusion
is vast.

No one ever tasted freedom, trapped
inside a box.
Freedom is the unrestricted leap.
The difference between a vault, and a vault
is vast.

Nothing is discovered by
pretending to search.
Pretense is a portent of
a life of wasted dreams.
The difference between sailing the tide
and staying tied to the dock
is vast.

Timid Reluctance is a sad
little town of wasted lives
broken chimneys, and excuses.
The difference between prevaricating
and prevailing

is vast.

                –Graves 11/19/21

Intention

Your strength is based
on clean intention.
Not clever lines
nor quick invention.
Your ability to exert your will;
and make things right
when the odds seem nil.

It rests on nothing as much, it seems
as your trust in yourself
and belief in your dreams.

–Graves 8/21/15

Kingdom of Dreams

Every dream is a pristine state
in the land of the possible.
Forming expanse and space within
a personal universe.
A spiritual land-form, already owned
aching to be walked. Pigments
of imagination upon the palette of he
who would paint the common universe.

One lives within the boundaries
of dreams and never outstrips them
without dreaming beyond them.

> -- Graves 11/7/15

Life as a Human

The bright orb breaches
the horizon; growing stronger
as it climbs. Sunlight
fades to moonlight
fades to starlight; and again

the sun rises.

That's how it works.

There are some who have been
so metaphysically abused, that
they become offended when they hear this.

Sunlight fades to
moonlight fades to
starlight. And

the sun rises.

That's how it works.

                    –Graves 11/25/16

Life is not a Death Sentence

Far from bridging the single span;
life, in truth, springs new from its own end.
Ouroboros in its eternal meal.
Life is not a Death Sentence.

As life prevails, we pass from one
frail vessel to the next.
Like the moon, which in eternal flight
both fades and swells.

This route has been the road for all
since once we chose this guise to wear
and will continue 'til we find
another part, which suits us more.

A part where Death's no longer
required, to spice Life's content
ringing down the curtain to entice
the crowd into crying out for more.

Death has never conquered life, save
in appearances alone. At most
inspiring fear in those for whom
clear mem'ry does not prevail.

They cling to that which seems to be.
And doing so, they feed their fear
of wretched death and dim in their sight
the fiery blaze of life!

Life is not a Death Sentence.
--Graves 12/4/21

On the observation of a cripple, yet buoyant.

The body is bent
the spirit is not, and pulls it
like a child dragging
some favorite blanket
from place to new place
looking for delicious candy.

–Graves 9/9/15

Path

Give one person a tool, and
they will use it
to change the world.

To another, that same tool
is nothing more
than a paperweight.

Decide to accomplish. And in that instant
the path to attainment
lies open before you.

It is there for you to walk.
It's up to you to see the path, and
gather the courage to walk it.

It is there.
But it permits no excuses.
Walk it, or don't.

If you decide to let it pass
don't then fall into regret.
For that will kill you.
Find the next one.

The right path
will pull at your feet.
And the walking of it will be
a dance.

–Graves 2/23/13

Quality (for Don Dewsnap)

There are many who settle
for the cards that they're dealt.
Content to gnaw whatever bone
lands on their plate.
Content to live the quiet, secure life.

There are fewer who seek
to better their lot.
To push harder. To accomplish
what others will not – sometimes
dare not, do.

They begin with a decision.
With tools and a purpose.
A canvas and a vision.
A chart that ends in the middle of an ocean.
A conjecture wanting for resolution.
With naught but a goal and
perseverance. And the drive to take it
beyond where before, it ended.

They begin with what is.
And form it into what can be.
They start with who they are.
And make themselves into what they would be.
They take "cannot"; and transmute it
by alchemy of will, into "can".

And upon these few
everything
depends.

                –Graves 9/6/15

Radiance

In the beginning, it seems just
a bright
light.

Most stars are

content to twinkle;
to politely sparkle
in the cool night sky.

Born sparkling;
that is all
the more to which they
attain.

Other stars
pierce the darkness, with
such

fierce
radiance

that the world is changed.

Brilliance is a natural
quality. Radiance, (as you know)

takes work.

But in radiance
lies the capacity to reach
into the darkness, and

to change the world.
–Graves 8/7/11

Note regarding the subject of the piece: Claude Monet (14 November 1840 – 5 December 1926); is called the founder of French impressionist painting. He painted what he saw; especially in his use of light. He was the most consistent and prolific practitioner of the movement's philosophy of expressing one's perceptions of nature, especially as applied to plein-air landscape painting. The term "Impressionism" is derived from the title of his painting "Impression, Sunrise" (Impression, soleil levant), which is regarded as the seminal painting in the Impressionist movement.

Monet and the other Impressionists fought an intellectual battle against the State-controlled art establishment in France, which at the time considered "French Romanticism" the proper expression of aesthetics in painting. The Impressionists ignored the ridicule of art "critics", the government, and large sections of the public; holding their own showings and continuing to promulgate their vision of a new way of looking at the world artistically.

Currently, The Impressionist School of painting is one of the most popular in the world.

Recipe (This is for you - today)

Every day
look into the next

and put at least
one
special thing
into that day. One thing
that you will enjoy doing. Your choice.

Something simple and satisfying. Or
complex and challenging.

Brighten another person's day.
Lighten another person's load.
Or not. Your choice.

Use this choice to bring a spark of light
to your day. Or (if you like) to make it a blinding
swelling, shining, sunrise of a day
which leaves your life changed – forever.
Your choice.

Plant a diamond in tomorrow.
Something that will make your heart sing.
Something that you will look forward to.
Something that makes you think
"That will be fun to do!"

And then do it.
And enjoy doing it.

You'll live longer.
You'll be happier.

                -- Graves 1/10/20

The Seeds of Illusions

I spent the first part of my life accepting
everything
I was told. It was truth. And so
I believed, without much question.
Fresh trust being what it is.

I spent the next part, knowing
based on these things
that what I thought
was right.
Just because it was what I thought.

Then, I found that
it wasn't.

And I began to see
that the truths which had
formed my life, were opinions, given
to masquerade as facts.
Opinion and truth: One fluid
One not.

And I had to learn - again

everything.

I found that much, seen through the lens
of acceptance and conjecture
was really mirage; constructed
in the service of
others who lived to control
and profit from the tangled vines
of the seeds of illusions
they had sown.

And – for me, with that – the world
changed. I saw.
Bits of actual truth among obfuscation.
Stars through clouds.

I had to tear apart and re-understand:
The world, and my place in it, my country,
my life, men and women, relationships,
honor and integrity, the purpose of religion,
lies portrayed as science, by
those who would hold sway.

All of this.

And I finally started to see.
And only at that point
did the chains begin to drop away.

--Graves 12/31/23

Slicing Tomatoes

I love slicing tomatoes.
Big, ripe, red ones.
Or heirlooms: Striped and colorful;
dense and juicy.

The knife needs
to be sharp, though.
Sharpen the right knife, and
slice them into paper-thin
wet, red pieces.

The secret is to let the knife
slide. Don't push it.
Let the knife do the work.
Slide it. And it slices right through
the firm, red
juicy
meat
of the tomato.
Let the knife do the work.

A lot of things are
like slicing tomatoes.

     –Graves 6/12/15

Space

You live your life in the space that you create.
Nobody else owns it.
Nothing else controls it.
It is yours. It exists
in tandem with the space
of others.
But it is yours.

You are free to move
or not.
Nothing stands in your way, unless
you elect it so.
(And then it's usually
for some entertainment purpose. One
of the hazards possibly of being
bored.)

It is: As high and wide
as broad and deep, as
filled with light or darkness
as rife with danger or with
sparkling opportunity
as you make it.

And you make it
simply by deciding that it is there.
Before that, it was naught.
After that, it is.

(Too easy, right?)
Light or darkness
mass or absence
matter not.
Up to you.

No one can interfere with it
unless you allow it. Which
you might, from time to time
and perhaps forget that you have;
just for the entertainment value of this.

The: "What!?!? How the hell!!!?..."
of it.
Entertainment. See?
But it is still your space.
And it interacts with
the space of others only
as you decide.

You don't have to believe it.
That's entertainment, too.
Your choice.

You create your life
in your own space.
Nobody owns it.
Nothing controls it
Except you.

And in your own space
nothing stands
in your way.

–Graves 2/18/17

Stuck

The will to do, is the child of decision.

Forgo decision, and you remain
rooted in the half-light.
Neither in darkness nor brilliance.
Waiting for a sunrise which never breaks.
Waiting for the night, shrouded in diamonds
that never falls.
And you will never
move.

What may become
does not.

And dreams
for lack of decision
die.

Decision is easy.
Move your hand.
Simple.

Getting to the point of decision can be
difficult; but never so toxic
as to sit and rot for lack of courage.

Decide.
Forward or back. Either
is better than no movement.
For in motionlessness, lies death.

Suspend decision, and you
remain in a holding pattern
circling the airport until
death runs you out of fuel, and
landing no longer matters.

Decision is the route from transfixed
to action; traveled in a flash.

All that is required is:
Decide
then Act.

There's the dime
you're on it.
GET OFF OF IT!

     --Graves 5/10/19

Notes: "Get off the dime!" An American idiom, meaning: to get started in some action; usually after a period of indecision or inaction. Originally, "get off the dime" was a term used by floor managers in 1920's dance halls, telling dancers to stop standing around and start dancing. Ten cents (a dime) was the cost of a dance. By 1926 the phrase had been extended to other activities. "Quit standing around! Get off the dime!"

Taking Off My Watch

Taking off my watch
I was finally naked.

No longer bound by time, and the feeling
that finishing
was urgent.

Trees grow
at their own rate.

Love wraps itself around lives
in its own time.

The Earth moves underneath me
at it's own pacing. Why

should I not do the same?

~Graves 6/28/12

Thanksgiving

Today, I am thankful.

For the rocky coast; the
challenging wind; the
circumstance that
makes me grow.

For the stars
which bid my vision
up and out.

For family, who warm my way
guide my steps
and make me a little
crazy, sometimes.

For friends, who
sweeten my life
with affinity.

For the one that I've
finally found, who
brings my life full circle.
And for falling in love
all of those times before.

For the child, who wakes
in the clear morning light
and is not afraid to see.
Who dresses the future
in dreams; and
graces the world
with wonder
and possibility.

For those who make the music that
fills up spaces in booming
joyous abandon or peacefully sings
the sparkling stars to sleep
in the night sky.

For the poet
whose words blaze with dreams that
inflame imaginations, kindle passions, stoke
the heat of life; and who paints with
rippling colors in the imagination
the road that takes us where
we have not been.

For the painter
whose vision spans the distance
between each of the separate
viewpoints of mankind
and joins them as one.

For the song defiantly sung, despite
suppression, and for those with
the courage to carry
the tune.

For those who walk
the lonely road
and keep the peace.

For the seekers of truth
and the dreamers of dreams
who return with visions
that seed the future.

For the clear, strong voice
which bends back lies with
simple truths, and drives out evil
like chaff before the summer wind.
That voice which vows to
never accept defeat.

And I am thankful for
those who come back.

They who are the
unstoppable
children of the wind.

And I am thankful
for those who share these thoughts.
Whoever you are
in whatever land
by whatever tongue
in whatever time.

For we share the same path.

–Graves 11/19/15

The Cliff

It is inevitable.
None escape.

For each soul, the nature of the cliff is unique.

A dark crag shrouded in thick, wet fog
towering in a windy sky.
A massive precipice overhanging
a gray, unfriendly sea.
A looming, vertical face of jagged rock
glazed by freezing rain.

You will scale it
or you will not.
You will best the fear
or you will fail.

The premonition of dire consequences
wearing down your concentration;
the wavering self-doubt, bound to your soul with fear
like the grip of an iron hand.

To the degree that they exist, you
have created them.
To understand that this is so
is the first step in ascending the cliff.

You will win most often, only
after you realize
that there is no reason that you need to fail.

Before that point, failure looms like
massive, hungry jaws
drawing you in, against your will.

Realize for yourself
that there is truly
no reason that you must fail;
and you will break its grip.

～Graves 3/3/16

The Mirror

There are many things
at which you've failed.
They will never change.

They're gone.
They've happened.

Revisiting them, repainting them
each time with fresh, thick, runny coats of
sadness, pain, and remorse; and then
preserving them carefully in a frame
beneath a shiny glaze of self-pity; won't change them.
The painting is never life.
It only somewhat resembles life.

Regret is a sticky pool of
sweet poison which serves no one.
Least of all, those you've lost.

You can't change the past
only your impression of the past.
The future, you change with each breath.

Do what you can.
Realize that what you did
was what you could.
And be at peace with that.

They've moved forward.
They're no longer there.
Neither should you be.

The future holds others with whom to laugh, and
with whom to create joy beyond past experience.
But to find them, you must move forward.
You must turn your gaze away from the mirror.

        --Graves 3/3/16

The New Year -- Angel Falls

The wet mists of Venezuela gather
and hang in the air of the high mountains, like
vaporous ghosts
strewn across the sky.
Like whispered ideas;
nascent dreams.

And in the air, droplet to droplet
they join, like seconds into
minutes; and fall on the high plateau.

Minutes trickle into
hours that flow into
days that join
and become weeks.

And at Angel Falls
they meet and

pitch-out-into-space, and fall

three

thousand

feet, as

rainbows and sparkling diamonds
in the sunlight.

As sheets of shimmer, and
pearls under the shining moon.

And nothing
is as it was.

And in the air, droplet to droplet
they join; and like seconds into minutes

they fly to the river.

                --Graves 1/5/17

Note: Located in Venezuela, Angel Falls is the tallest waterfall in the world, with a vertical drop of 3,212 feet; 2,648 of which is freefall. It takes a while for the water that leaves the top of the falls, to hit its base. Angel Falls is not fed by a lake or a body of water like most waterfalls, rather it is fed by rain that falls on the mountain plateau from which it descends. It comes from the clouds.

The Past

The things at which you've failed
will never change.
They happened.
They're done.
End of story.

Revisiting them and
repainting them each time with
fresh, thick,
runny coats of sadness, pain
and regret; and then
carefully
preserving them beneath a shiny glaze
of sympathy; will
not repair them.

The painting is never life. It only
resembles life.

You cannot
change the past.
The future, you change
with every breath.

Regret is a stagnant, misremembered pool that
serves no one, except those wishing
to drown.

Do what you can.
Realize that you have
done what you could.
And be at peace with that.

Living in the past
serves no purpose.

The future holds others with whom to laugh
and to create joy beyond
past experience. But
to find them, you must move
forward. You must turn
your gaze
from the past.

    --Graves 9/8/17

The Taken Road
(with gratitude, to Robert Frost)

I may have mentioned this before
but there are times in life, I think
when every poet wonders if
the road not taken, might, perhaps
have been the psychopath.

Yet, paths being – obviously – what they are
he wonders to himself how far
he'll be allowed to run the road
he's chosen for himself, unbowed.

And when at some point time's embrace
becomes impossible to elude in the chase
will its arms be icy cold or hot?
Though, in the end it matters not.

For with each new beginning, there's always been
as plain as day, an earlier end.
And no matter the times we've run this road
from end to end
it always (always) seems new and strange
when we set foot on it once again.

–Graves 6/12/15

Version 6.1

I see so much
more now.
Still marking the transition from
looking to seeing. But

I know now, that I know
less than I thought I did. But
more
than I actually did.

The perspective is simpler.
Because there is no longer any
getting away with
pretending that things are
not as they are.

Solutions are more
obvious, yet less (it seems)
easily embraced
by others.
With certain exceptions.

I have found a clarity
which was murked, earlier
by well-vested assumptions that
there was no more
to know than
what little was known. And
that's why things seemed so
much simpler.
Smugly drenched in confidence, dripping
impercipient certainty of
correct assessment.

I lacked the balance of
the more complete
picture, to check
forward motion (which
was at times
a bit off-kilter.
Or a lot.)

Caught up in the irretrievable forward thrust
"All hands to the barricades!"
The cry, stained in blood-lust and expedience,
which now - when I hear it - seems
so much tinsel-drama and avoidance
of a real solution; requiring sagacity, and
navigation.

The throbbing tango, which
bereft of true insight into
the other, is
simply a quest to
spear or be speared for
no more reason than
avoiding boredom, loneliness, or
the acquisition of notches. Though
a notch, in the end,
is simply the creation of
a void.

"Do not go gentle into that good night"
but do
get the fuck! out of my way
with your irrational
nonsense!
The view from clarity (such as it is)
is too beautiful, too
serenely stunning to share
with vampires who live
in a state of inconsequential drama-lust.

In them, I see too much
of my earlier self and
shudder with familiarity, hoping
that they might avoid
the feces in which I stepped
earlier on the road.

I see so much more, now.
I know that
I know
less than I
thought I did, but more
than I actually
did.

          -- Graves 8/17/13

Poet's Note: I wrote this in the year that I turned 61, Hence, Version 6.1.

Wake-up Call

Choose too soon and you will miss
the one for whom you wait.
Wait too long and you will find
the hour has grown too late.
Either way, keep well in mind
it's never up to fate.

Move ahead or stay behind
the choice is up to you.
The universe is waiting now
to see what you will do.
Sit too long just pondering
and you will miss your cue.

I've left this poem here for you
a message from the past.
These verses are a little nudge
to not let wonders pass.
Just a word, make use of time
as water fills your glass.

A little nudge reminding you
TO GET UP OFF YOUR ASS!!!

                              --Graves 12/15/15

Prescience

You'll never find a place to live
that's quiet and safe and warm.
If you dedicate your life to trying
to right all wrongs, by storm.

But as I watch you swing through life
so bold and brave and free,
it makes it clear that safe's not how
you want your life to be.

> --Graves

THE VINCENT SERIES

The Unquiet Mind (Vincent No. 1)

I paint
the canvas
of the unquiet
mind.

I paint
the un-still life.

I paint

peasants wedded
to the earth with
brown
knotted roots;

carving

colors with
deep
turns
of the brush.

Carving colors
into

Swirling
piercing! stars.
Powerful, twisting!
winds.
Trees
that struggle to break
loose!
from the earth.
Crows
in flight.
I see

the un-still
life.

I see
people
drinking-in the
colors! guzzling
life from shining
stars in a (deep, deep blue)
Rhone-night sky.

I see
the un-still life in
its thundering brilliance!

Reds! greens! indigoes! midnight blues!
and always the yellow! always
the chrome
yellow.
Life bleeds!
Life explodes!
Life creates!
or life is
nothing.

Nothing . . .

I would rather writhe
with riotous whores
than tiptoe
in the
timid
chastity of the
fearfully correct.

For one rips!
away the covers
of life
and the other hides . . .

fearfully
in hopes of its
avoidance.

sigh

What is seen
as madness, is
sometimes

not mad

but simply
life
spoken
in a different dialect.

Life
which, in the look back
takes shape, like the
brick-red
end of a
caboose
receding in the distance.

Paris - City of
Light -
too dazzled
by its own narcissistic
glitter, for too long
to see
the un-still life.
And nothing sold.

To see . . .
sigh

And now I sit
carving colors

out of words
waiting for the crows
once more
to take flight.

With a handshake
Ever yours,

Vincent

              --Graves 2/4/11

The Night is Still (Vincent No. 2)

The night is still . . .

not cold
not warm
the air is wet
and thick.

There are no
sounds
except the quiet river
and the movement
of the air.

Standing near the grove
I can smell
the giant cypress trees
breathing.

The light
of the bright moon
is on the hills.

I can feel it
drenching the earth.
Radiant waves swirling
through darkness.

Stars pin the dark heavens
to the sky.

I can feel their light
on my skin.

I see shadows – like
dark paint running
down canvas to drip
on the wooden floor
of my room.

Like blood
minus color
in the night.

Eyes closed, I sense
the turning of the Earth.

Paul does not
comprehend.

He thinks I like
to fight with him.
In truth, I just live.

He cuts the depths too
shallow for my taste.
He'll only graze the surface.

He is scared
in the end.
Scared of the edges
of his personal canvas.
Scared of the depth of

the un-still life.
The life that moves
on its own.

The life that must
move on its own.

I see
the field of winter wheat
spectral-gray
in the moonlight.

The crows are sleeping.
I must paint,

before the darkness
consumes me.

With a handshake,
Ever yours,

Vincent

                --Graves 7/11/20

The Focus of Madness – (Vincent No. 3)

The world is filled
with light!

Like a shimmering bowl.
I see
what I see.

I stare into the dark.
And it moves like air
in the night. And I see
what I see. And
I am told,

I am mad.

I have found solace with the Roulins.
Someone
cares.

Armand cocks his hat
in anticipation.
The crows dance
their stately dance
on the red tile roofs of Arles.
They know.

Exquisite beauty balances precariously
a bare breath away from becoming
mundane.

A shift in the eyes
a shunt in the mind, and
beauty tumbles into trite.

To remain still
is to rot in the hopeless stasis
of the uncommitted.

To lose the jouissance;
to strip the light! and colors! and fire!
and sensation!
from the life that breathes --
that burns! The "inappropriate"
life which tears!
free! from channels! of supposition, and dances!
on its own; even
though, in dancing, it risks
falling onto
the sharp rocks. Life
is not still...

Brilliance shines from a ragged
rip in the fabric, pierced
by truth. The light
shines forth from
the place where
those: Quietly proud
of their mercilessly mundane lives
dare
not
look. Because

the light
is too bright.

Their focus is too weak
to tolerate the brilliance
of the glare.

Truth be told
it shines only as bright as it truly is. No more.

What they call madness, perhaps, delves
with one hand
in the realm of common experience. While
with the other
picks
jewels from the sand
in the other realm. The

realm that wraps around
the colors which
in their brilliance
blind weaker eyes.

Focus...
there is always

focus . . .

on what?

On that

which others see
as madness . . .
sigh

They focus only
on the easy.
The apparent.

They fear to focus beyond
what is real to them. That focus
is perhaps, not such madness as
they would believe;
but simply the view which they will fear
until their eyes
become accustomed
to the light.

I will continue to paint
until the sun sets.
And then, I will
paint the night.

With a handshake,
Ever yours,

Vincent

                      --Graves 3/30/13

Definitions:

Jouissance: Physical or intellectual pleasure; delight; ecstacy.

The Roulins: The Roulin family served as friends and models for Van Gogh during his time in Arles. It was difficult for Van Gogh to find models to sit for him, yet, in the Roulins, he found an entire family. Van Gogh and Joseph Roulin met and became good friends and drinking companions. Van Gogh compared Roulin to Socrates on many occasions; while Roulin was not the most attractive man, Van Gogh found him to be "Such a good soul and so wise and so full of feeling and so trustful." Strictly by appearance, Roulin reminded Van Gogh of Russian novelist Fyodor Dostoyevski – the same broad forehead, broad nose, and shape of the beard.

Armand Roulin: Armand Roulin was born on 5 May 1871 in Lambesc. He was 17 when portrayed by Van Gogh. Perhaps the most famous of the portraits of Armand Roulin, depict him in what are likely his best clothes: an elegant fedora, vivid yellow coat, black waistcoat and tie.

Wheatfield with Crows (Vincent No. 4)

The Muse has taken

flight.
On massive
golden wings. Into a
darkening,
night sky.

The back of her head
is all
I now see.

And the crows.

I am very

tired.

I have danced
this mad, frenetic dance with
Her
for five years.

And I am

spent.

The spells come more often when
I feel
I have nothing
left to say.

The emptiness is
dark
hollow
and deep.
It stains me
blue/black like
the wide, night
sky.

The horrible void in me
where she now
is not, is filled
with

lonely nothing.

It passes
but it always
returns.

And each
time
it deepens.
It claws at my throat
like the death of
a friend.

I have endured
this madness long
enough.

The road ahead leads
'round a corner

I cannot
see.

She has changed my eyes to
see things I do not know
but which belong to
me
alone.

And now they feel
blind.

She consumes me
with brilliant colors which
I can only borrow and
convey; and I am
running out
of paint.

I am running . . .

out of paint.

With a handshake,
Ever yours,

Vincent

--Graves 3/4/11

Poet's note: Lines 1—10 of this piece are a description of the painting "Wheatfield with Crows." Look at it and you may see the same.

In his lifetime, Van Gogh sold only a single painting: "The Red Vineyard at
Arles," to a friend and fellow artist. His career showed life in a brilliant, sensory light not before seen. A little over two weeks after finishing "Wheatfield with Crows," Van Gogh died from a gunshot wound. See my piece "Epilogue" for insight into this incident. I believe that recent forensic evidence has revealed it to be more than has been publicly portrayed

He was 37.

Epilogue (Vincent No. 5 – Van Gogh did not kill himself)

After the sun bleeds out
its colors into night.
After the flesh grows cold.
What remains are simply stories.
Receding memories, dimmed
by the bright light of the present
and by the hope of a future.

Absent the corporeal husk,
the vision gains an acuity
elusive in life.
I ask you:
Why would I have killed myself?

It is true, there were days
when it felt like
the Muse had left me
and would not return.
Days of crushing desolation when
all that remained was the lonely
emptiness of hell.
Days when the road ahead turned
a corner, beyond which
I could not see.
But it was not always thus.

And not on that day!
I had paints on the way.

The world was learning to see!
Finally! To see the un-still life.
The life that moves!
There was a review written. In Paris!

The world was finally
opening like an iris on the
cusp of Spring. Sunlight coaxing
diaphanous petals from a
tightly clasped bud after the long,
frigid desolation of winter.

They say that I shot myself.

Absolutely not!
A Mortal Sin!
I was too long a student of the Bible
for that. My first calling - before heeding
the siren's song of the Muse - was learning
to preach for the Lord.

I had paints on the way.
Theo was sending paints!
The summer was exploding
with subjects! Sunlight
trading light and dark with clouds
in gusts, like the raucous laughter of the drunk
who suddenly sees the holy vision
denied to more timid souls.
So many things to paint!

Suicide?

An adolescent would-be cowboy* walks
the streets of Paris.
An accidental murderer
in the French countryside.
He and his brother were my friends.
At the beginning of their lives.
The pretend cowboy, then fleeing
Auvers-sur-Oise, mid-season as though his
guilt might be outrun by flight.
An outlaw in the American west, fleeing
town on horseback.
An imagined posse in pursuit.

And the stories began . . .

Emile is brilliant but always looking
to turn the trick.
Always the opportunist.
He promotes himself first with my ear
then with my death.
I bear him no ill will
for a painter must eat.
And he is my friend.

Gachet's son, weaving tales
to suit himself. The location
of my death was his idea.
In truth, I was on another road.
The road from the house of the cowboy.
Not in the fields.

And Adleine, with her stories:
What does she know?
She was only 13 when it happened.
Her stories were from Gustave, her father.
Gustave, who surely thought, "Mais, bien sur,
the crazy dutch painter finally
killed himself. Everyone knew
that he would someday."

Friends and acquaintances, all
condemning me to Mortal Sin,
by assumption.
Because of course,
Fou Roux was crazy.
It was an easy answer.
"Of course . . ."

All that is left of me now
are paintings and letters.
Memories -- context, long
obscured in the haze of time.

I leave to you
the un-still life.
For I must move on.

With a handshake. Ever yours,

Vincent

      --Graves 1/17/15

POET'S NOTE: There remain many unanswered questions regarding the death of Vincent Van Gogh. The movie "Lust for Life" (1956) starring Kirk Douglas, painted a dramatically popular portrait of the artist. There is evidence, however, to indicate that they got Vincent's death wrong.

There is a lot that doesn't make sense about the "Vincent committed suicide" theory. The gunshot wound was in the wrong spot for a self-inflicted wound. Forensic review indicates that -- based on the description of the wound as reported by the two attending physicians -- the gun was fired at some distance from the skin; not in close proximity, as it would have been were the shot self-inflicted.

Van Gogh's final letter to his brother Theo, which he had posted the day of the shooting, July 27, 1890, was optimistic, even exuberant about the future.

Van Gogh was wounded – very painfully - with a pistol. If he had shot himself, why not just finish the job on the spot with a second, better-placed shot; rather than make his long, painful way back to the inn where he was staying?

Van Gogh's painting equipment was never recovered, nor was the pistol – as it probably would have been – had he shot himself in a field next to a haystack, as reported by Emile Bernard.

*The reference to "an adolescent, would-be cowboy" refers to Rene Secretan, who was 16 at the time of Van Gogh's death. Rene was the son of a wealthy Parisian pharmacist, whose family summered in Auvers. He had been influenced by Wild Bill Cody, whose wild west show he saw in Paris. As a result, he purchased an American cowboy outfit, including a small caliber pistol.

Rene and his teenage brother Gaston sometimes hung out with Van Gogh; reportedly talking about art, playing pranks on the painter and sometimes consorting with dancing girls. It is easy to imagine a very plausible scenario in which the two teenage boys and the artist are horsing around with Rene's pistol which went off, delivering the fatal wound. And Vincent perhaps not wishing to destroy the lives of the two boys, then took the blame for the wound upon himself.

GLOSSARY:

Emile: Emile Henri Bernard (April 26, 1866 – April 16, 1941) A French Post Impressionist painter. A friend of Van Gogh, Paul Gauguin and others

Gachet: Dr. Paul-Ferdinand Gachet (July 30, 1828 – January 9, 1909) A French physician and amateur painter. Dr. Gachet was a great supporter of artists and the Impressionist movement. Known for treating Van Gogh during his last weeks in Auvers-sur-Oise and for being one of the two physicians overseeing

Van Gogh in his final days. His son was Paul Gachet Jr.

Adeline: Adeline Ravoux: The daughter of Gustave Ravoux, the owner of the Ravoux Inn, where Van Gogh was staying in Auvers, and where he died. Adeline was 13 at the time. She did not speak for the record until 1953. When she did, she mostly channeled the stories her father, Gustave, had told her half a century earlier. Her story changed constantly, developing dramatic shape, and even dialogue, with each telling.

Fou Roux: French: "crazy redhead" Van Gogh's nickname.

LOVE

The Secret to Good Sex (a modified sonnet*)

To seek the grail seems less involved than the secret to good sex.
Though many seek and seek and seek and end up as miserable wrecks.
They pen the things that work for them and end up sounding sappy.
If you want to solve the secret, simply sleep with someone who's happy.

Sleep with someone miserable, and you'll end up stained with gloom.
You'll wake in the morning and find that they simply want you out of the room.
The sex was bad, their life is bad and you're now the brunt of complaints.
Conveniently, you're near at hand, though by now you're wishing you ain't.

A train wreck is a joy compared to sleeping with someone unhappy.
Give it a shot and believe it or not, your life will be nothing but crappy.
Take this course and you'll live a life that's laden with regret.
A safer and more joyous game is classic Russian roulette.

If all you know are happy folks, it's far less problematic.
Unless, of course, you misconstrue and they're actually sociopathic.
If you'd care to test my premise and pursue it to its conclusion,
You'll find that it's an easy one that results in little confusion.

The answer then is simple and your life will be quite snappy.
If you just make the person you're sleeping with extremely, delightfully happy.

--Graves 12/30/14

*Notes: I kind of "bent" the form on a sonnet in this piece. A Shakespearean or English sonnet consists of fourteen lines written in iambic pentameter, a pattern in which an unstressed syllable is followed by a stressed syllable five times. The rhyme scheme in a Shakespearean sonnet is *a-b-a-b, c-d-c-d, e-f-e-f, g-g*; the last two lines are a rhyming couplet.

Often, the beginning of the third quatrain marks the volta ("turn"), or the line in which the mood of the poem shifts, and the poet expresses a revelation or epiphany.

In this piece there are four quatrains instead of three, the volta occurs in the fourth quatrain, it's written in iambic septameter instead of pentameter and the rhyme scheme is aabb, ccdd, eeff, gghh, ii.

I bent the form a bit.

Woman

Too often man lives doomed. In love
with beauty alone. An image
woven in sensation, expectation and
delight. Of equal parts vibrant thoughts and
immortal expectations; like
some wondrous, conjured creature sprung
full-grown from sorcerer's brew:
A dash of impossible
a pinch of unattainable, simmered
in unimaginable beauty
brought forth before the shining moon
to wander Earth for him alone.

Bereft, he lives
unable to paint into reality
the portrait, large enough to
encompass the scope of his imaginings. Never
realizing that the sweeping size
of his expectations
is far
too
small

and far
too
over-thought
to fit
the truth which
awaits him -- but not

forever, should he but see
what is there
and what is not
and
in comprehension, begin
by saying, simply "Hello".

The only hope that he has
is to not die before realizing
that worlds beyond splendor are his
for the taking, should only
he grasp
this
single
concept.

              --Graves 10/3/14

The River

In my life
I swear, I will know you.

I will know the soft, wet
moss, surrounding your delicate
trickling wellhead.

I will know each
of your myriad moods
mirroring the terrain
for hundreds of miles.

I will know
your boisterous, triumphant entry
to the sea.

I will glide
the length of your
twisting
course
dipping my paddle
again and again

into your cool
liquid current
as I pilot my boat
between your smooth
slippery banks
to find your hidden
eddy and quiet ripples.

I will ride your wild
bucking rapids until
spent at last
with heaving chest
weak from exertion
I emerge triumphant.

Drenched from your
wet embrace.

I will race your twisting
length, flying wildly
before your current
like a leaf in a storm.

I will chase the reflection
of the running moonlight
along your banks
in the cool spring night
beneath sparkling stars.

And I will know you again
and again, until finally

you carry me
home.

    --Graves 1/15/14

The Whisper of Sheets

What was it you said?
"I'll stay with you, until
the season turns
and then I'm gone."

And I thought: "Eternity is
only the amount
of time that we possess.
No longer than that, matters."

An entire lifetime is simply
a line of dialog in a play set in aeons.
A play completely enveloped
by each of us, in a far
longer game, forgotten
by so many.

One lifetime spent
is the snap of a match, igniting
in the night; its light changing
the landscape in ways
impossible to foresee. Yet
even before the light, we knew
all that the night held.

In the darkness
I feel you breathing.
This temporary eternity is all
the time that I need.

I hear, in the whisper of sheets
a thousand voices
that I have heard
constantly for as long
as I have been listening, and
that I have heard once and never again.
Each speaking of a separate voyage.
Each voyage a single
life. A discrete path with countless
potential branches through future.
Hinged only on choice.
All of them – and none
of them – with you.

The night looms
long. Empty in the fullness
of space contained
in unpopulated dreams.

In the darkness
I feel you breathing. I hear again
the whisper of sheets.

This particular eternity is a drop of time.
Temporary, like a handful of rain.
Temporary, like a handful of rain.

–Graves 3/26/21

This Morning I Stayed in Bed (for Holley)

This morning I stayed in bed
with you.

I kissed your face.
I smelled your hair.

And felt your warmth
in a way that
I had not
before.

This morning I stayed.
And a different future opened.
And my eyes opened.
And I saw a place that
I had never been.

Promises to others
I left strewn across the bedroom floor
to pick up
at another time.

This morning I stayed.
And watched you breathe.
And with each breath
the outside world felt farther
and further away.

We watched the leaves.

We fed the cat.
And every little
thing
was right.

Because this morning I stayed
with you.

    --Graves 2/13/15

Love Match

To us, it was a game.

Immortal then
twenty and nineteen and drifting.
Passing life at breakneck speed.

I wrote
and lived for music.
She captured the world
on film.
A skater, her blades carved
my dreams.
And from those carvings came songs.

And we studied.
And we played
in tandem on a blissful run behind
the Gates of Eden.

Our life was chess, and chess is life
(minus, of course, the unexpected change of rules
by pieces.)

Every night
at dinner - two alone
in a noisy, crowded college cafeteria.

Our board and
our armies of 16, we sat

eye-to-eye
blue to brown
joined at the board.
A different plane.

Conversing in moves.

Pawns advancing
one step
at a time
to meet pawn.
Slowly savoring
each step
of the erotic pavane.
Making the most of
each move.
She'll "take" on a diagonal
or from behind, if the other is quick enough
to pass.
A slow mover, but transcendent
in the tango of the end game.

King's knight is prancing.
Out early.
Cutting corners to get to
The Show.
Moving in all directions
hoping to get some
satisfaction.
Flashy riding.

Queen's knight charges
recklessly in and out
defending all at once
from every corner.

Cool and distant
she claims, to the end
until she too
in heated lust of battle
is captured.

The tall bishop
with his heady crown
always waiting. Always yearning.
Poised for the incisive
long
diagonal
strike.

Rooks trembling with eagerness to escape
their defending pawns
and get some action of their own.
Always the escape artists.
But once only.

The nimble way she used
her knights
enthralled me.
Her lascivious look as queen took bishop.
Positioning - always positioning
in the dance.

For an all too short nine-month eternity,
we waged.

Until at last
I looked up from life.
With a flash of crystal insight.
And saw the sprite across from me
commanding an army.
She castled

And I was left.
Downed king and empty chair.
And the game.

Too fragile to last
too tough to be forgotten.

No chance of mate.

     --Graves 3/31/17

Glossary:

"Gates of Eden" is a reference to Bob Dylan's song "The Gates of Eden", which was written about the time that he spent in college.

Again . . . (A love song)

Night comes.

The wind blows.

Time, with its many songs, enchants/distracts
even the most intent listener
weaving its ribbons, like dark tendrils
deep through memories.

Tried as I could, to keep
my thoughts of you alive
with time, memory paled.
Until I'd lost you to songs
that could not be denied.

Time had spilled the fact of us
drop by drop into a
foaming sea, churning with currents. Yet

at the edge of awareness
where perception walks the bridge
into imagination, I felt your presence.
Sensing only, that beyond
the clouds covering the night sky
a star secured my way.

The fact of you, concealed
amorphous like mist on water; yet
indelible as the color of my blood.

All that time.

Then, as if time had been
cut away by a sliding blade of sound
I heard a cadence of intonation.
A phrase.

Words, mirrored from a forgotten
part of consciousness.
Echoes through time. The casual turn
of a forgotten phrase
suddenly familiar.

A personality that weaves with mine too
precisely, too intimately
to be chance.
And those eyes – mirrors
of eyes that I have known
and loved like no others.

There is no mistaking this.
This is not just chance encounter.
The light of recognition
shimmers, then glows.

You know it, too.

                --Graves 8/28/23

Beauty

Beauty is that of which
when you encounter it
you must drink deeply.

There is no escaping this.

Your eyes draw me in like this.

The delicate folds of the iris in bloom
a diaphanous petal balancing a bead
of dew in the morning sunlight
refracting the colors of both.

The hawk riding thermals
motionless yet moving.
Gazing out from height
to the ends of the Earth.
Eyes that miss nothing.

I look away, then look back
to drink more deeply.
Then look away.

When I look back there is
always more.

Your eyes draw me in
like this.
                    --Graves 1/1/15

Courtney

If way exists to get it done
she will.

Little did I realize (at first)
my youngest had cut a deal
with the universe and it lost.

Yet, she finds snails and squirrels
delightful company. Go figure.

The secret (and benevolent)
Queen of the Universe talks to snails.

And for all I know, they talk back.

Do you need a building built from nothing, in Italy?
A galaxy strung with stars?
Old news... already done.
(Yes, really . . .)

And why do I sense that was just for practice?

Her effortless intention could burn holes
in the sun. (For my sake I hope
she doesn't take THAT on as a project
on some cloudy afternoon.)

How could I live without this sprite.
This effortlessly competent hero.

This player of vast games.

We're rushing the barricades!
("What barricades?" she says . . .)

How she does this, I have yet to fathom.
I guess there just are no barriers
at the edges of her personal universe.

                -- Graves 5/21/10 rev. 9/10/21

Crystalline -- A love story in three small parts

You . . .
whew!
Who knew?. . .

...wheeling,
reeling,
looks revealing.

Hocus pocus,
altered locus,
new focus.

Too fast,
too fast,
it'll never last.

New position,
listen,
glisten.

Kiss, bliss
always miss
will persist

We go
just so,
great flow.

Saw you with 'im
Sensory prism
sudden schism.

Inquisition,
supposition,
bad decision.

Stupid
Cupid!

Pine,
pine,
pine...

Pine,
pine,
pine...

Contact
react
is that a fact?

Confrontation
explanation
revelation

New position,
listen,
listen...

New locus,

regain focus
. . . regain focus

crystalline. Ahhh . . .

You . . .
whew!
Who knew? . . .

              --Graves 3/16/10

Erin

My little one,
my middle one,
my stubborn one.
Radiant as the sun,
holding planets in their place.

Sparkling fairy, quite contrary.
How does your garden grow?
Trying this, trying that,
posing in a cowboy hat.
Backbone of titanium.
Makes me crazy, sometimes.

My shining diamond
in the rough.
Comes out swinging,
laughter ringing,
lightning zinging.
Life will never beat you down.

Sometimes I think
that she doesn't know
she's already won the race,
to my heart.

--Graves 12/30/14

Eye of the Beholder

Beauty is a thing which whispers
from the past.
It permeates a person present or a thing
like light on a screen and imbues
with a remembrance upon which
you cannot put your finger
but which resonates from
within the similar form before you.
A remembrance, which once
filled you with awe or love.

From whence comes our consideration
of the beautiful? Beauty being
"in the eye of the beholder," and varied
as it is among us, as are individual
sparks of light, flashing
from a shining, cut stone.

Is beauty a piton, solid in the rock face
of the wall of life, or
is it a reflection of that which
in its spark resonates?

Is beautiful a misted memory of melody
or vision of that which once inspired and
evoked passionate victory when
victory was that on which
everything depended?

Love is a different thing from this. Perhaps.
And sometimes, something on its own
is simply beautiful.

Is aesthetics a conjunction with
that memory-personified vision which wakes
you in the night, rekindled
with the surging strength of a past joy?
That thing you search for in the eyes of
people passing in a crowd? The exquisiteness of form
the delicacy of design, the heat?

It perhaps is all of these
and therein lurks the danger.
For truth is beauty but beauty
is not truth. Perceived perfection
of form is not perfection of soul.
Porcelain skin, regardless of hue
striking eyes, a strong jawline
and muscular, tanned arms.
None speak to character.

Lies can be concealed in the blinding light
of a beauty, in which we by feelings
are compelled to believe.
Deception, hidden within the most
ravishingly beautiful form.

Know this and you will not fall into
that trap which reaches to capture you
with beauty
yet hides a blade.   --Graves 2/14/23

"Gerunds, Verbs, a Couple of Adjectives and an Adverb"
(List 1: 59 words)

[To be savored not rushed.]

... looking

wondering

waiting

lingering

hoping

talking

touching

joking

nudging

laughing

longing

meeting

kissing

smiling

caressing

breathing...

breathing

holding

stroking

warming

moistening

deepening

damp

holding

swelling

rubbing

tweaking

licking

sucking

swaying

rubbing

dripping

plunging

rocking

breathing

harder

rolling

bucking

panting

squeezing

moaning

gasping

grasping

arching

thrusting

spasming

twisting

turning

breathing/breathing

breathing . . .

slowing

sighing

smooth

dripping

smiling

breathing . . .

. . . looking

wondering

waiting . . .

                --Graves 11/27/15

I Loved You More

I loved you
more
before
You started using my face
as a testing ground
for arrows.

                --Graves 2/5/17

Last Night in Houston

Outside, the cold Texas moon moved
slowly higher, eclipsing each
burning star in her path.

Inside, we lay basking
in a place just outside
of time. Where we
danced our dance on rough
white sheets, then slept in the
night heat, drenched in moonlight.
Savoring the urgent hunger.
Waiting for the deep, pulsing beat
of the music to resume.

So soon to be apart (again)
the anticipation of leaving, sharpening
the taste. Sweetening the bloom.
We danced the fevered dance of dreams.
Our pasts and futures as transcendent
and fleeting as the blinding fire
of skyrockets, burning an image
in the retina, and then
vanishing in the night.

I was too drunk on
love. Too deaf to see.
Too blind to hear.
Too hormonally bound to a journey
with a destination made possible, only

by delusion. In truth, it was my
willingness alone to be blinded and bound
by lies, that spun the trap.

My gift to you, you said that night, was
the grant to finally see
your long-denied dreams
as worthy of pursuit.

And you left. Knowing.

Your gift to me, in the end
was a vast, empty space
in the cold night sky
to soar and look
down upon the Earth.

                        -- Graves 11/27/21

Lingerie

Skin moves beneath silk.
Fabric covering, yet not.
Power is revealed.

--Graves 2/2/16

Merchants of Small Wars

"The first thing we do, let's kill all the lawyers."
(Dick the Butcher, Henry the 6th, Act 4, Scene 2 --
William Shakespeare)

The playing finally
stopped.

The last echo
of music died away:
sucked into solid, reliable
well-used walls.

The band packed up its things.
Our dance, which had begun
with such riotous abandon
was finally over.

We parted.
Speaking acquaintances

knowing that there would not be
another dance.

No more summer nights.
Not a good
night kiss left.

And we proceeded to begin
again, to cut
our own separate paths.

Love, long ago, had bled out,
into now-dried pools
on a stained, kitchen floor.

Perhaps we wished then, to leave
some dignity intact;
some humanity for things
gone tragically wrong.

Perhaps, not.

In any case, it was not to be
allowed;
for waiting at the door
briefs in hand, were the merchants
of small wars.

Vampires of the emotional night.
Condemned by choice to stalk the
dark, decaying side of human existence.
Feeding on the detritus
of dead and rotting love.

Sucking what life-heat remained
from the embers of hatred.
Fanned by their sly, foul breath.

Pandering physicians of
perniciously-strengthened, vengeance.

Setting half against former half.
Completing the cleave
of what, once, you said could never
be broken.

Fanning flames of malice
with surgical precision into a searing hatred
not known in the wars of State.

Seeking not to heal
but to take.

"But we are only establishing agreements
to allow life to continue!"

"We are the merchants of small wars.
you will divide, and we will prevail.

And settlements will be made..."

                      --Graves 5/3/19

Missing Pieces

I heard the door shut.
And in the quiet afternoon
I exhaled.

I closed my eyes.

The time when I could have said your name
and made you pause, had passed.

The day edged past.

In the silence of absence
things change.
Pieces which had once so
smoothly fit, now tug at me
in their dissonant absence.

Your empty chair.
The feel of your skin, moving
against my lips. Your taste
on my tongue.
Your missing laugh.

Your warm breath on my neck
in the dark.
Your small smile, as you dreamt:
Delight, behind closed eyes.

Your smooth back rising
and falling in the half-light.
You slept.
The smile in your eyes.
Clear. Bright. Missing nothing.

The perfume that lingered on my shirt
in the morning, after
you removed it.

Your toes.

My back pocket misses your hand
as I walk.
My ears hear
the missing echo of your step.

I find that I am missing
pieces.

      --Graves 9/23/16

Mountaineer (to Jaxon)

The clouds finally part.

And I see you
in the distance
on the mountain above me, waving.
Like some intransigent diamond
set amongst
the rocks of time.

For you have chosen
the vertical trek
where life is win or die.
The holy light of purpose shines
from your eyes, brighter
than the fiercest star, as you climb.

On a course so few have seen
as yet, or even dared
to imagine, you
industriously plot your way beyond
the line of human sight.

Focused on the rocks above.
Seeking out the next vantage point
from which to reach
a place
closer to your own
eternal sky.

You will reach bounds beyond
any to which I hope to aspire
just now
my son.

And someday (I know) you
will find a way to sink a piton
into clouds
and just keep climbing.
Where others would have
long since sought
the descending trail.

It's true, I take another path.
A chimney in between the rocks
while you hammer
piton after
piton into
the living rock
of the mountain
and continue to
ascend its unforgiving, icy
face.

No man resembles my dreams
so much as you, my son.
And somewhere
up the mountain, we will sit
out of the wind
around a fire.
Anchored for a time
to rocks of our own creation.
And share stories of the climb.

                --Graves 1/23/15

Pre-Houston Rush

Probably not
a hundred miles out
I'll start to feel it.
I'll smell your perfume
coming from
some nowhere
I'll feel you
snuggle against my chest.
Arms around me
and hear you chuckle.
I'll feel your smile.

Feel
your smile.
And my whole
life
re-ignites.

    --Graves (Somewhere in the air.
      Sometime in 1994.

Road Map

You may get tired of hearing
that everything in my life
leads back to you.

Or maybe not.
You see, there are a lot of
roads on this map.
Lots of roads.

Decisions.
Confusing damn thing...
And I really can't read it
too clearly in all this wind
and rain.

I've been sitting here for hours
trying to plan my trip.
Hours.

And I still can't figure out
which way is North.

Then you grab my map
fold it up
grin at me
pick a direction, and point
and we're off!

                    --Graves 4/6/18

The Sidelong Glance

She sees him. Quite
by accident.
Her eyes widen.
And she turns away.

She looks again.
Just a glance.
The glimpse like
sipping rich tawny port.

Each taste tantalizing.
Satisfaction, coupled with
an aroused plea for

. . . just one

More . . .

Each glance concisely constructed:
A lick.
A taste.
A small but deep intrusion.
Each a brief
politely hooded sip.
So as not to consume
all at once
and leave
the glass standing empty.

Each sip savoring the
fleeting flavor wrapping itself
around her tongue. Its tendrils moving
slowly downward
drawing her like gravity, to
the deeper fire.

She lightly licks her lips
and sips
and deeply breathes again -- savoring.

He rises and leaves the room
and the fire
does not leave with him.

      --Graves 5/5/17

Smile Today

Starts like a sunrise
out over a clear blue sea.
Lights up the clouds in the sky first,
and then it hits me,
Stunned like a ton of bricks
hit me from out of the blue.
I look past your beautiful smile
and see only you.

--Graves 4/13/09

Note: This is a little ditty that I wrote by request for a friend who was starting up a dentistry-related business.

Sunday Morning Interruptus

One too many distractions
in a beautiful morning: It's like

eating mochi-covered ice cream
for the first time.
You pop the whole thing
into your mouth and
it's kind of exploding with flavor
and cold, and someone insists
you drink some hot tea: right now.

It's lost.
You never get it back.
Don't drink the tea.

      --Graves 5/4/19

The Air

You are oxygen to my flame.
Without you, I do not burn.

In your absence
though the night carries no concealing clouds
there is no light.

You are the riotous wind
that stokes the ocean to a frenzied rage.

The breath that silently forms
ripples on the mirrored pond.

You are the air that slides across
my skin in the sultry
wet night.
Lighting fire.

You are the air.
Without you I do not breathe.

      --Graves 5/25/13

The Buoy

In the beginning, she starts out slowly.

An easy rocking
so as not
to cause
too much
alarm.
Gathering momentum
she starts to move
faster, higher.
But the storm is not
quite
yet.
She has time.
And for now she is only
rocking, rocking, rocking.

The passionate, cold moon higher now;
wet, and covered with wet
in the cold night she bucks high
on the heaving swell; And
down again she rides the smooth

wet

slide

deep

into the trough, again and again and again.

Moans of the foghorn coming close
now fainter
now closer, cut through the deepening fog;
warning of danger to be avoided.
Entanglement to be avoided.
The price of involvement too high.

Up
and down!
Up and slamming down!
The slap

slap

slap

loud and wet in the violent, dark night.
She knows that, for her at least
this is Not an entanglement.
Just a ship.
Just a ship passing in the dark, dark night.
Its wake driving her dance harder, faster, harder!
The gathering mists shutting out

all

perception

except the motion.

And the frenzy of the coming storm.

-- Graves 4/8/17

The Fool/The Blindness

And then at some point, older
perhaps than you'd imagined;
you'll see yourself, in your mind
in some familiar place, that
you once frequented with aplomb.
[Once - when you were just so wise.]
Facing a massive wall of stone blocks, which
stretches to the right and to
the left, farther than you'll
allow yourself to turn your head, to find
a way around it - listening
to silence, where there
should have been laughter.

Recalling the lies that you told yourself.
The governing misconceptions that
you've hugged preciously to yourself, all
these years; which have kept you
bound to the path which you have
by their election, chosen.

A love wasted. Simply
because of something you
did not care for in her face.
Or the way her knees looked when
she stood just so.
Or the single patch of cellulite on her thigh
that marred your precious moonlight.

You stand, recalling the depth of affection
that you let fall into the
dark crevasse of time. Lost
like some dancing, festive balloon
cut callously loose on a windy
moonless night. Cut with the blade
that you've used to glibly slice so much
out of your life. Simply because
it was there to be wielded.

This wall will obscure your
view of anything else. It will
block your path, until
you allow yourself to decide
to turn in another direction
and see the open future.

Until you allow yourself to
take a different path
you'll stand there
staring at the anchoring
stone blocks of past confusion
and regret. Keeping them rooted
in the present by your
decision to allow yourself
to look no farther.

Until you decide to fully look at them
and understand them
and then turn your head
and walk away;
they will not be behind you.

Turn your head and walk forward.
It's up to you.

>   --Graves 1/29/21

The Sea

She is the sea.

Lounging languidly;
recumbent and shiny
beneath the hot, azure sky.

Not a care.

Across a tan stretch of sand
soft and wet
she pulls me deep into her
sensuous, undulating waves.

She is the sea.

Her tides: high, low, rip, ebb, stand, red, flood, neap...
I will never
know all of her moods.
Nor understand.

But there is no need.

She is the sea.

She rages before
the winds of
change.

Holding to her own rules, bending
to the will of none.

Her tide ebbs, and
she is sharp rocks
barnacles and
slimy green things.

She is the sea.

I sail her
with my smooth, wooden boat.
Its hull dipping
between her
heaving
swells.

Her rocking, wet
slap
slap
slap
against my
wooden hull
leaves my bare
wind-burned skin
soaked
and wanting more.

She claims neither
responsibility nor care
for my attention.

She is the sea.

Capricious and
frisky in
white-caps, she sparkles
shimmering, wet moongleam
in the night.
Awaiting my return.
Feigning disinterest, yet
waiting
to be
engaged.

And She is the sea.

--Graves 3/24/18

Tips From My Father

My father was an engineer.
He gave me tips along the way.
He told me, "Work while you're working, son
and play when it's time to play."
He said, "They'll wonder after you
and ask which way you went.
If, in every job you do, you give it 110 percent."

–Graves 1/7/16

Note: This piece is dedicated to my father: Douglas C. Graves. The best man I've ever known.

Today I go to take back Houston

Today I go to take back Houston.
To eat where we ate.
To sleep where we slept.
To make our places
my places.

I still can feel
the sliding slice of the blade
when you decided we would be two.
You made wielding it look effortless.
Almost matter of fact.

I like to think – looking back
that in the severing
you were also cut.
The pain, perhaps yet to arrive
with dried blood left in crusty
flaking bits around the wound.
But perhaps you were not.

I thought that I heard
the sharp intake of your breath
weeks ago, when
your practice blade accidentally slipped.
I thought that I heard
the pain in your voice. Saw the blood
in a dream.

Two days ago I set aside my strength
and wept.

Today I go to take back Houston.

>   --Graves 1994 - revised 5/18/17

Tonight

Tonight, the dead will remain dead.
And we, my love
aloft with life, shall reign
vibrant and shining, while
breath remains within us.
Glowing like two coals born of
incipient fire, bathed in recombinant light.
Memories of another time
sent to a place away, and told
to be still.
For tonight, the dead will remain dead.

                --Graves 6/7/14

Travel Guide

You may get tired of hearing
that everything in my life
leads back to you.
Or maybe not
and wonder why this is.

My life is a map
with lots of roads.
Lots of roads.
Confusing damn thing.

I sit here for hours
candle in one hand
compass in the other
trying to plan my trip.
And I still can't figure out
which way north is.
And it's difficult to read
in all this metaphorical
wind and rain.

Then you you grab my map
fold it up, grin at me
pick a direction
and point.
And we're off!

And that's why.
         --Graves 8/26/17

What to Send Railyn and Kiara for Christmas?

We sat and thought
and worked our brains;
we thought in cars,
we thought in trains,
we squinted our eyes,
we scratched our heads,
we thought about it at night in bed.

Something for Christmas
for two girls so special
is a serious thing
so we wrestled and wrestled,
with ideas so silly
and some that were bright
cause we really wanted
to get this thing right.

We thought about it
an awfully lot
and didn't want you
to think we'd forgot.

And after a while
we finally got wise
that no one could pick
a better gift than you guys.

So here's what we sent
we hope you enjoy it.
We hope that you'll take it
right out and employ it
to get something happy
that only you'd think of,
and know it's from us,
with a whole lot of love.

Love and Merry Christmas (in February),

Mike and Holley

You were simply gone – To Dylan, Baez, and the rest of us.

Young and running with the tide.
It seemed that God was on Our Side
We never found our place to hide
and honestly, I didn't want one.
The shore back then was far away
safety in a sheltered bay.
I just never cared enough
to swim there.

I know now that I misbehaved.
Too much pressure, I simply caved.
So much was lost, God knows what saved
me from the endless fall.
I couldn't see at all.
But by that time
you were simply gone.

And on that day when I awoke
face down in a gutter, nearly broke
you'd grabbed a taxi, never spoke.
I was so alone.
My thoughts were frozen, to the bone.
And you, my White Queen
you were simply gone.

I lay there breathing, so bereft
you'd hit me with a killer left.
I was left gasping from the theft

just lying on the ground.
No pieces to be found.
I'd been living in my head, and
you were simply gone.

I thought I'd been on solid ground
but standing there, I turned and found
that there was nothing else around
that anchored me like you
to understand the view
it all had gone askew.
And by that time
you were simply gone.

It seems so cheap now
for me to say
some line best meant
to throw away, like:
"The two of us were just not meant to be."
I was far from free.
Wrapped up in being me.
It took me quite a while to see
that you were simply gone.

Since that time
I've heard from friends
that this is how a story ends.
That something breaks
but something bends
and carries on anew.
Please don't misconstrue
I still search my mind for you

because inside me, you're
not simply gone.

              – Graves 8/21/18

POET'S NOTE:

This piece is written in Dylan's lyrical style.

In "Chronicles: Volume One," Bob Dylan's 2004 autobiography. he wrote that the first time he saw Joan Baez on TV, "I couldn't stop looking at her, didn't want to blink... The sight of her made me sigh. All that and then there was the voice. A voice that drove out bad spirits... she sang in a voice straight to God... Nothing she did didn't work."

"With God on Our Side" was the first song that they ever performed together, at the Monterey Folk Festival in 1963. Baez and Dylan were together for two years from 1963 to 1965; and during that time they graced the world with a starkly uncommon beauty. A combination of diamond drill and angelic grace which did much to usher in a period of massive social change in America.

Baez left Dylan midway through their 1965 European tour. When asked about that breakup in the Martin Scorsese film "No Direction Home," Dylan paraphrased Francis Bacon, saying of himself "It is impossible to be both in love and wise."

MAGIC

Reminder: Magic

Within all of that of which you can conceive
lie all of the paths in which you can believe.

All of those things in which you can believe
are also the things you'll find you can perceive.

Anything that you decide you can see
you also will have the power to be.

The decision you make about what you can be
is also the magic that sets you free.

Your decision's not only the key to the map
it's also what gets you outside of the trap.

-- Graves 10/31/20

Glossary:

Conceive (verb): 1. To hold to be true, by decision or by discovery.

Decision (noun): 1. The intentional selection of a pathway in an infinite non-linear group of potential experiential possibilities; the contents of which are limited only by the considerations of the decider.

Perceive (verb): 1. To know, discern, identify, recognize, understand through any medium of perception, be it physical (e.g. hearing or sight) or metaphysical.

Life's a Mystery

Life's a mystery
'til you unlock it.
Just pick up the diamonds
and put 'em in your pocket.

 —Graves 2019

QUESTIONS

Why Are We Here?

A friend of mine once said to me
that he wasn't really clear
on the reason behind existence,
on the answer to: "Why are we here?"

Are we here to forge a cleaner soul,
to take our turn at bat?
To wrap ourselves around a pole,
and learn great things from that?

Are we here to learn great truths
and tip the scales to balance true?
Are we here to keep the game in play,
to give Karma something to do?

Are we here to find the perfect match
of fortune and true love?
And to find out after searching
that they rarely go hand in glove?

Are we here to cook the perfect batch
of some outrageous dish?
Or grant a dying child the right
to have his perfect wish?

Are we here to solve deep mysteries
that make the world go 'round?
(If a tree falls in the forest, alone,
does it really make a sound?)

Are we here to differentiate
minutiae from profound?
Or thinking, transubstantiate
our way out of the ground?

And having done so, will it mean much,
as one's life unwinds;
to solve the deepest mysteries,
to find the greatest finds?

Now I suppose, to some degree
these things have some import;
and some of these will give one peace,
if only of a sort.

But really, when the course is run,
how much of it will matter?
See, one might save the universe, or
be trapped by senseless chatter.

To make a choice between these paths;
which one will carry true;
is truthfully the only thing
of value to me and you.

It's not a stupid question, though.
I've given it some thought.
The answer my friend,
to "Why are we here?"
may simply be: "Why not?"

–Graves 2/3/12

Musica Proxima Etern*

If you listen closely
you can hear, without your ears
the harmonics of aetherial* variation.

A complex range of nano-sounds
so tightly bound yet separate, that they
form a context much like starlight singing.

Gravitics bend the resonating
notes you hear inside your head. Their melody
composed of the refracting light of stars.

They resonate with sounds, much like
a hundred thousand angels playing
pitch as pure as starlight, light as dreams
and deep as darkness.

All these sounds, and so much more
are ambiently present. Like the single-dripping
line of water lost in sound, among the rain.

Moonlight fills an empty room
and overcomes the darkness.

And as it fills the emptiness
it sings.

-- Graves 9/19/20

Definitions: *Musica Proxima Etern: The First Music of the Eternal

Aetherial: Pertaining to "aether" According to "old science" aether (also spelled "ether") is the material that fills the region of the universe between planets, stars and other extraterrestrial phenomena. The concept of aether has been used in several theories to explain natural phenomena, such as gravity and the transit of light between source and effect in space. In the late 19th century, physicists postulated that aether permeated all space, providing a medium through which light could travel in a vacuum.

It is interesting to note that the concept of ether was considered disproven by a single experiment conducted between April and July 1887 by two scientists in Ohio. While this experiment has been replicated since then, and forms one of the acceptance points of special relativity, I believe that it missed the mark. If mass warps space by its presence – gravitically-caused or not – what does it warp? Space, by definition, would be an empty void. There needs to be something there, in which to create the warp (or well) experienced around gravitic objects. I may be wrong, but then, I also think that Darwin offered "an easy answer" which was accepted and forwarded by pompous academics, from the safety of university classrooms, who never got out there and looked. Darwin's math doesn't work either. See my piece "The Easy Answer" for explanation.

Travel: In-between the Ticks of Time

There is little that appears
more godlike to man than time.

One man takes a lifetime
to accomplish little.
Another man changes
the entire world.
Both live within the same hours.
But one has far more time.

Thought requires no space.
Nor is it regulated by time.
Doze off for just a few seconds
and you might fall
into a very
very
long dream.

Time is a frame of reference.
And because we believe
that it is beyond our control
we accept that we cannot
influence it.

The least godlike thing
is that thing which we can easily
understand and control.
To some, a flashlight is magic.

Focus
and create twice as much
in a single moment.
(Not a minute - a moment.)
And you have just (to some degree)
doubled time.

Focus
Now create three times as much
(not frantic, not frenetic:
triple content)
and you have tripled time.

How much time can you create
operating in this fashion?
I can't tell you.
But I can tell you
that it will be more.

Once you've gotten used to doing this
then decide
to complete something
in less time than it "should" take.
Or decide
to arrive at your destination sooner
than should be "reasonably" possible
(without speeding).
And then do it.

It takes practice.
(Though interestingly, not effort.)
You may notice only small changes
at first.

But once you've seen
those small changes
You will see, that
larger things are possible.

In your own time.

                --Graves 5/20/17

The Easy Answer

Okay, let me get this straight.

You start with a really
really big, sterile rock
spinning in space.
It's got smaller rocks.
It's got water, heat
light and dark
It's got gases surrounding it.
It's got no life.

Then, over a very, very long time
this pile of sterile chemicals racing through space
(no dirt, because dirt requires vegetation
and it's got no vegetation)
combines and recombines in
every possible combination of the available
rocks
water
heat
atmosphere
light and dark.

Mind you, there is no starter mixture
like you need for a good sourdough bread
or yogurt or kefir or a nice cheese.
There's no decaying organic matter from a forgotten
compost pile or stagnating swamp (there's nothing to
stagnate).
None of that.

And what you're telling me, is that
over hundreds of millions of years of
sterile stuff, plus
sterile stuff, plus
sterile stuff
you get a really big rock spinning through space
covered with intelligent life – to say nothing
of a myriad of other, wildly divergent
life forms?

And you get this
with no outside interaction of any sort?

That's like saying "If all you have to work with
are 1's and 0's and you stack them together in an
infinite array; at some point you are going to
spontaneously get a 3 or a 7 or a 9."
Because you happen to have a 3 or a 7 or a 9
and you think you're going to look bad
if you can't explain how it got there.

Here's a similar question:
If you dumped a million sterile marbles a day into
a lifeless ocean. How long would it take
for Leonardo da Vinci to
come striding forth from the waves;
to just come walking out of the ocean
...surfboard in hand?

Does it seem like there's
something missing in this equation?
I'm not necessarily saying it's God
and I'm not necessarily saying it's not.
It's just that there has
got to be something else
going on here. You
can combine all of the dead chemicals that
you want, and you're not
going to get something that's alive, Okay?

It's a lazy, clueless approach.
And it disingenuously, conveniently leaves out
the fact that life
does not come from non-life.
Life comes from life.

It's like having an F5 tornado run through a huge
junkyard
of scraps, and leave behind a working airplane.

It's an easy answer.   –Graves 6/13/15

Why we do what we do

We create.
In order to grasp a clearer sense of that
which stretches out behind.
And from this sighting, spot
those points which help us plot
a course along the path which lies ahead.

And what is this trip, but
sensation and adventure? What is life, but
a search for realization and amazement
among the round, gray rocks
of an eternal seaside? An
entertaining side-trip into a realm
where we imagine ourselves as not
all-powerful and omniscient?
We create.

If you wait for the Muse
to bequeath you your gift
what you desire will never arrive.
We create.

If, along the road, you see
the diamond of your dreams, it's up to you
to draw it close
or pass it by. It's your diamond.
Why should it matter
to anyone else what you do with it?
Until you do with it
what you will.
And upon that, for someone else
may rest everything.

We create.
The future
lies only in the realm of magic.
For nowhere else is it to be found.
It is only as
you create
it. And how else
would you describe magic?

Naught but memories inhabit the past.
Nothing living to be found there.
You may as well search the eyes
of those you see along the way
for the ghosts of lovers who have
long since left the room.
Many do. And live lost in the search.

We create.
We dance on metaphysical toes
across a very personal universe.
We do what we do
for love of the dance.
And for the entertainment.

                –Graves 10/18/16

A Little Ado About Nothing

Today, I wrote a poem about something
that left out nothing.

And since nothing was left out
it feels a little lacking
because it's all about nothing.

I'm wondering now whether or not
I should have added nothing more
about nothing
or added something more
about nothing.

It's difficult to say.
Because nothing, being a somewhat slippery thing
is hard sometimes to grasp.
After all, nothing... is nothing.

On the other hand:

When you do nothing,
you're really doing something
by doing nothing.
And then again, when you do something
you're not doing nothing.
Unless, that something is really
nothing at all.
In which case, it's nothing.

Nothing, after all, is important.
If there was no nothing
how could you walk in-between something
and something?

How could you separate this and that
if there was not nothing
between them?

So, nothing is not without consequence.

Look all you want, and you can't spot nothing.
Because clearly nothing's there.
So actually, you can. But only if you realize you're
seeing nothing, and that there is
truly nothing to see.

As I said: Today, I wrote a poem about something
that left out nothing.
This bothered me a bit, because
the subject was also nothing.
A balancing act over nothing? Perhaps.
It's possible, though, that I'm simply being
overly concerned about nothing.

                    --Graves 7/31/15

Aliens're Comin'!
(Lyrics . . .
. . .in the talkin' blues tradition . . .
. . . with humor) ;-)

Aliens 're comin'! Hey, don't frown,
they're comin' soon to your home town.
Comin' in Vimanas, comin' as blips,
on radar screens in saucer ships.
You'll see, before too much time passes,
we'll all be up to our dear, sweet asses
in Aliens.

My ma ran by, she was all delirious
I said to her "Don't be so Sirius
They come in colors other than gray
You'll see em sometime, any day
they've got big eyeballs, long skinny arms
They grow 'em new on alien farms.

Right down there with the broccoli. . .
In cabbage patches . . .
Somewhere on the moon . . .
Cute little sprouts . . .

I don't know, but many say
they're gonna be here any day.
I'll tell you, if I had my way
I'd band 'em up and teach 'em to play . . .
guitar... (You seen them fingers?) . . .
the five-string bass... the tambourine. . .
they'd make wild drummers . . .
(But that's just me.)

They're visitin' Giza, a great ole time,
an' ogling them big Nazca lines.
They're all out there getting satisfaction
at all the alien tourist attractions.

Stonehenge. . . the pyramids. . . Carnac. . .
Checkin' out Roswell . . .
Rockin at the Macchu Picchu Hilton . . .

I've seen 'em partyin' wild an wacky,
dancin' with the Anunnaki.
Doin' hand flips, splits and drops
carryin' on, they just don't stop.
I'll tell ya though if it gets outta hand
You'll find me in an alien band.

Playin' rhythm . . . Makin' tips . . .
Hangin' with the short, Gray kids . . .

                --Graves 8/9/14

Sequential Glossary:

Vimanas: (Plural of Vimana) Ancient flying machines referred to in the Ramayana, one of the two great ancient Hindu epics. the vimana of Ravana, King of Sri Lanka, is described as follows:

"The Pushpaka Vimana that resembles the Sun . . . was brought by the powerful Ravana; that aerial and excellent Vimana going everywhere at will . . . that chariot resembling a bright cloud in the sky. . . and the King [Rama] got in, and the excellent chariot at the command of the Raghira, rose up into the higher atmosphere.'"
It is the first flying vimana mentioned in existing Hindu texts. Their design, function and operation are seen by some as evidence of extraterrestrial intervention in early Indian culture.

Sirius: The brightest star in the night sky. In some ancient cultures, Sirius is considered to be the home area of "gods" who traveled to earth to impart knowledge.

The Dogon people are an ethnic group in Mali, West Africa, reported to have knowledge that was handed down over generations which would normally be considered impossible for them to obtain without the use of telescopes. For example, their knowledge of the fact that Sirius is a double-star; a fact not discernible with the naked eye. Therefore, a fact that they could not possibly have discovered on their own. That, coupled with their use of ceremonial costumes that bear remarkable resemblance to suits worn by astronauts have lead some to speculate that the Dogons had interaction with extraterrestrials in the distant past.

Broccoli: A green vegetable that your mother probably tried to get you to eat. But you probably already know that one. ;-)

Giza: Giza, Egypt – Location of the great pyramids, the Valley of Kings, and other structures for which mainstream archeology has found insufficient explanation . . . It's a long story.

Nazca lines: (Ref. Nazca, Peru) – Google it. This refers to ancient pictures drawn on a high plateau in Nazca, Peru that are so gigantic that they can only be viewed in their entirety from very, very high in the sky; raising the question of who drew them and who were they drawing them for?

Stonehenge: A prehistoric construction in England. Built between 3000BC and 2000BC. Really big, really heavy stones. Set up in ways that many people say that a hunter-gatherer society at that time should not have been able to do.

The pyramids: Though there are many remarkable pyramids on the planet in both hemispheres, the pyramids that I was referring to here, are the three pyramids at Giza.

Carnac: Carnac, France the site of an array of nearly 3,000 massive stones, erected in straight lines sometime between 4000BC to 3000BC. Unusual because – according to many authorities – a culture just coming out of the stone age would not have been capable of nor organized to the degree that they could have created this monument.

Roswell, New Mexico: Site of a UFO crash in 1947. After being reported in a local newspaper, the crash was the subject of a subsequent, massive cover-up by the US Government.

Machu Picchu: Famous city built by the Incas, high in the Andes.

Anunnaki: The Anunnaki are ancient Mesopotamian deities whose name means – according to some - "those who from the heavens came to earth", and as such are suspected of being extraterrestrials.

Grays: also referred to as "Greys" and Roswell Greys. The origin of the idea of the "Gray" is commonly associated with the Betty and Barney Hill abduction claim which took place in 1961. The Gray aliens are also famous from the Roswell UFO incident of 1947.

Angel Wings

Angels don't have wings.

Wings are a marketing device
that makes them easier to sell.
It also makes it much easier
to avoid the paparazzi if people think
you're supposed to have wings.

Wings stick out in a crowd.
A stylish affectation.
Angels don't need
wings.

Do you actually think
that a being like that
would need wings?

I mean
Really . . .

They would only get in the way
in elevators;
in small, fast cars.
They would be a nuisance
in a movie theater.
You'd have to keep them cleaned . . .

Do you know how involved it is
keeping wings clean?
Birds do it, bees do it
They've got nothing better to do.
Preening, preening, preening . . .

Wings.
Humans need wings.

It's a good thing that most angels
have a sense of humor.

If you're going to look for angels, watch
for the radiance
not wings.

Wings. Really . . . ?

     --Graves 11/28/15

POET'S NOTE re: Angels and wings: I did some research on this, and while angels are normally portrayed in art as having wings, the Bible normally presents them as appearing like men (i.e. no wings). In the case of Abraham, three angels appeared to him and at first he thought they were men (Genesis 18:2). Similarly, when an angel appeared to Samson's parents, they thought he was a "man of God" (Judges 13:9-10). Hebrews 13:2 says that some people have "entertained angels unawares," indicating that they appear as ordinary human beings.

Sometimes angels appear in white. Examples are John 20:12 and Acts 1:10; but wings are not mentioned. Wings, being pretty noticeable would likely have been included in the description, were they present.

There is one passage which describes an angel in "swift flight" (Daniel 9:21), but again no wings are mentioned. And, in any case, there is no reason to think that a being of such spiritual advancement would need wings to fly.

There are two angel-like creatures that do have wings, and this may be the origin of the idea that angels have wings. Cherubim (Exodus 25:20; Ezekiel 10) and Seraphim (Isaiah 6), which are both described as having wings. However, these are not angels.

I don't raise these points in order to be contentious. You are more than welcome to subscribe to the "angels must have wings" premise. After all, who's to say that a creature of that level of ability might not don wings, should the notion occur to it.

Breathing

The narrow river winds across
the Venezuelan high plateau
its path lacing worn sandstone outcroppings
to clumps of towering ferns.
Time meanders in this place
governed only by the sun
and by the moon.

In the concrete-colored sky
a hawk circles slowly
riding thermal currents
marking time in terms of food.

Is time the rings in the heart
of an ancient tree? Is it
the number of heartbeats
between sunrise
and winter? Is it
the number of human lifespans
in the migration of a field of lichen, across
a granite escarpment?

"Time is a standardized measurement
of the stream of existence."

Or is it?

There is time;
and there is the behavior of clocks.
One is the mechanical harness
the other the flow. And, no.
They are not the same thing.
One is rigid. One
is fluid.

Gravity – it turns out
affects time.
Speed (approaching light)
affects time.
Ask a quantum physicist.

Consciousness (also)
affects time.

Time, then, tends (it seems) toward the tensile.
Clocks, perhaps -- not so much.

If a tree fell in a forest and
there was no (actual) tree
would there be
time?
And would it
matter?

Time expands
or contracts
depending on how you look at it.
The slow-motion instant
in which your car spins
out of control
into oncoming traffic.
The brief span of time
in which you accomplish
an amazing amount.

The passing flash of an hour when
you're not paying
attention.

Clocks measure ticks
with spinning wheels
crystal oscillations
dripping drops of water
slipping grains of sand.

Is it the ticks and tocks
that sound the holy notes
of this song?
Or is it the rush (or pause)
of the conscious stream?

Does time come in two flavors?
Mechanical and
metaphysical? Or is it like
vanilla chocolate marble ice cream? Both
constituents dependent upon
the other in a Yin versus Yang swirl?

Time is not simply
a mechanical man breathing.

                     -- Graves 10/27/17

Farside Traveler

Stand her on her tail and
KICK IT!

Heavy G's and all.

Straight

up

into

the

thermosphere

(She'll do it in 28 seconds -- 32 max. My beautiful arrow.)

The sky gets dark.

The stars get bright.

You brink the atmo, and head
for emptiness . . .

Why call it space?

Don't know.

Why not call it
area?

Maybe it's that other dimension.
It's long. It's high. It's wide.
And it's mostly empty.

Empty enough to lose pieces
of your soul

to the vastness

and never get them back.

                 -- Graves 3/3/16

Gaia (Clues to Existence)

Neither deity nor mortal, she
permeates the clear sky.
Cloaking herself in verdant fields;
in vast, azure spaces
in future.

Traces of her presence abound:

Off Queensland
along the Great Barrier Reef
I have seen a thousand shining fish
rocketing through the sea
turning and twisting as one synchronous body
on the timing
of a heartbeat. As though
directed by a single intelligence.

I have seen ten thousand bees
one loud, thrumming, buzzing
hive-mass traveling in unison, all
turn on a dime
again and again
as from a single thought.

I have seen five hundred birds
flying soundless in an
overcast, empty sky
veer sharply - as one - to avoid

nothing I could see

and then arrive
in the same beat
on a new heading.

I have seen three hundred thousand
multi-colored Baikal Teal
blanketing the Siberian sky;
moving as one, toward Korea.
A single, massive cloud, so thick
that it dimmed the sun;
layering the tundra in shadow.

Have you ever seen a murmuration of starlings?
Have you seen the way that they move?
If you haven't, you should.
This is not 10,000 separate birds. This is one huge
entity crossing the sky.

Think of these things
and then, think
much
bigger.

And that is Gaia.

Earth teems with life. Yet
for so many reasons
there should be only death here
were dice truly being played
with the universe.

If the sun alone held sway
even with atmospheric protection
the Earth would be a barren crust
coasting in silent, dead circles
through space. Burned
free of all life.
The temperature though
instead of fatally rising
is somehow cooled
and maintained.

In every ocean, the massive
volume of poisonous salts cast off
by Earth should combine and collect
making one vast toxic soup
deadly to life down to its very cells.
And yet, they have not.
The oceans balance and cleanse.

Oxygen: A chemical both tempestuous and
promiscuous, second in this only to fluorine
should have combined with other elements
and fled the air we breathe; coupling
with chemicals in the crust of Earth
like some hungry, wanton whore
leaving us nothing.
Yet, it has not.

Balance has maintained.

Gaia's presence is spiritual, not
synaptic; And looms so far and
closely-woven through
all of this particular
piece of creation
that it is like oxygen.
Unnoticed

until it is gone.

Perhaps the evidence of
Earth's singularity is not simply
the presence of life.

Perhaps it is a larger life form
within the space of Earth
that has given it a different function
than the dead celestial bodies.

Not God, per se, but an encompassing
spiritual presence maintaining
the balance of those factors allowing
the possibility of life.

A presence felt; not seen
save in effect:

The wide, wide, deathly-silent
tree-lined, rock-walled canyon that
inspires reverence.

The massive desert, stretching
beyond bounds, with space so deep
that it fills to the brim
with awe.

The broad expanse of restless, sleepless ocean
that beckons with promise
of the unknown, yet
imbues with caution.

The swarming air mass, churning
in a seething storm, birthing
monstrous, towering clouds that billow
huge and dark before your eyes
and bring the exhilaration of a spring rain
and deafening thunder.

Neither deity nor mortal
Gaia permeates the clear sky
and cloaks herself
in verdant fields
in vast, azure spaces.
In future.

--Graves 6/21/20

Glossary:

Gaia (noun): In Greek mythology, Gaia was the personification of the Earth, one of the Greek primorial deities. Her equivalent in the Roman mythology was Terra. In this case she is seen as the spiritual influence which maintains the Earth, its systems, and life upon it. It seems evident, however, that she may not be particularly particular about what that life consists of at any given time.

The "Gaia hypothesis", also known as "Gaia theory" or "Gaia principle", developed by James Lovelock, PhD. and microbiologist Lynn Margulis in the 1970's proposes that organisms interact with their inorganic surroundings on Earth to form a self-regulating, complex system which contributes to maintaining the conditions for life on the planet. My thought is that perhaps there is a metaphysical aspect to this. Not "God" per se, but a motivating, spiritual force which has assumed responsibility for Earth and which seeks to maintain it as a bio-retentive environment.

Gaia* Rising

Gaia seeks dynamic equilibrium
and ignores all else
except the turning of the time.

Her movement toward balance
is inevitable.
Unstoppable.

Twelve thousand years ago
the fifth ice age ended.
Glacial ice fields
two
miles
thick
binding the northern hemisphere
like a frigid shroud
melted.

Sea levels rose four hundred feet.
And consumed ten million square miles
of dry land.

Mountainside became seaside.
High hilltops became islands.
Valleys became bays.
Ranges of mountains became archipelagos.

Gaia speaks
in the thunder
of the tsunami swallowing the shoreline.

She whispers
as fog quietly strumming
blades of grass slides
down wet, green hills.

She murmurs
as the small stream cuts
its way into the face
of bedrock.

She sings
as the tornado dances
and whirls wildly in the night.

She laughs.
And in the earthquake
a range of mountains
changes.

Wind moves through needles
in the mountain grove of pines
as She sighs.

Ignore Her at your peril.

    --Graves 6/26/20

Glossary:

*Gaia (noun): In Greek mythology, Gaia was the personification of the Earth, one of the Greek primordial deities. Her equivalent in Roman mythology was Terra. In this poem she is seen as the spiritual influence which maintains the Earth, its systems, and life upon it. It seems evident, however, that she may not be particularly particular about what that life consists of at any given time.

The "Gaia hypothesis", also known as "Gaia theory" or "Gaia principle", developed by James Lovelock, PhD. and microbiologist Lynn Margulis in the 1970's proposes that organisms interact with their inorganic surroundings on Earth to form a self-regulating, complex system which contributes to maintaining the conditions for life on the planet.

In the Gaia series, I posit a metaphysical aspect to this. Not "God" per se, for the premise of God is far more extensive and permeating than this; but a motivating, spiritual force which has assumed responsibility for Earth and which seeks to maintain it as a bio-retentive environment.

Dynamic equilibrium: The state in which balance is maintained in an evolving system. Equilibrium is a state in which balance is maintained as a result of all acting influences being canceled by others; resulting in a stable, balanced, or unchanging system. Dynamic equilibrium posits a similar state of balance in an active, evolving meta-system composed interacting systems. Balance is maintained within an environment of movement and evolution. Much like riding a bicycle.

Geography

North, South, East, West are
directions made for an Earth
once thought flat -- before
it got wrapped

around

a sphere.

Quite adequate for making your way across town;
or for sailing a wide, icy polar sea.

Lacking in dimensions, though, for plotting
the truly interesting course:

In which direction lie dreams?
In which direction lies birth?
In which, death?
Where is last week?
Where is your kiss
from once?
Where is the time
we spent lying in the sun?
The time that we spent laughing
in the dark; breathing; spent?
Which direction do I travel
to get it back?
To return?
Or to move forward?

The dervish whirls, but
does not travel.
Thoughts run rampant. Yet never
leave the spot.

Waves wash against a foreign shore, yet never
leave the ocean.
The hawk flies high and straight.
Between the clouds.
He crosses the mountain with ease, yet never
escapes the sky.

In which direction is beyond?
In which direction is tomorrow?
In which direction is next?

      --Graves 12/8/17

God is a Mirror

God is a mirror
which
already knowing the joke
smiles back
in appreciation.

               --Graves 7/29/10

I am not my chair

I am not the stories
I tell.

I am not the songs
I sing.

I am not the poetry
I write.

I dream
but I
am not my dreams.

I believe
but I
am not my beliefs.

I think
but I
am not my thoughts.

I am not my accomplishments.
They will stand
without me

I am not my history.
It is a trail
behind me.

I am not my hands.
They are useless
without me.

I am neither the uniform I wear
nor the
causes
for which I fight.

I am neither the car I drive
nor the king
I serve.

I am neither my bones
nor the meat package
in my skull.

The problem with forcing
the answer to everything to fit
into the framework of what is
already known, is
that nothing new
is ever
discovered.

Supreme conceit:
"The Earth
is the center of
the universe."

"Blood flows through
the body because
of tides."

"Man will never
fly."

I learn from my mistakes.
But I am not
those mistakes.

What I have been taught
has changed me
but I am not
those teachings.

I am eternal
and I
do not age.

I am not
my chair.

–Graves 2/18/17

Messages in a Bottle

"...The Stone Age ended circa 3,300 BC, with the introduction of bronze tools. The earliest evidence of written language dates from 2900 BC. Scientific advancement of any significance, though, was still more than three thousand years away..." -- *Anon.*

"When I look back at all the crap I learned in high school. It's a wonder I can think at all..." -- *"Kodachrome"*, Paul Simon, *songwriter*

A cool breeze blows the morning sunlight
into a million piercing, glittering points
bouncing off a million dancing waves
on the eastern coast of Yucatan
between Cancun
and the western tip of Cuba;
in the southern doorway between
the Caribbean Sea and the Gulf of Mexico.

Right there. Right now. On the sea floor

two

thousand

feet

down, lies a city built of carved stones
each weighing tons. Where
the laughter of children
once rang happily in the streets.
And lovers lingered in convenient shadows
creating light.

More than six thousand years ago
this city was consumed by the ocean.

This city is a message.

Eighteen thousand years ago, icefields
two miles thick, covered the northern
and parts of the southern face of Earth.

Twelve thousand years ago, the last
of the five ice ages ended.
The planet warmed.
The glaciers melted.
And the waters came.

Ten million square miles of a spherical Earth
dry and fertile for tens
of thousands of years
were swallowed by the sea.
Coastlines changed radically.
And messages were left.

Nine thousand years ago:
Three thousand years before
there were pyramids at Giza.
And forty-five hundred years before Stonehenge
the two hundred and three massive
"Speaking Stones" of the Karahunj Observatory
stood on the high plateau of ancient Armenia
and plotted the stars for five thousand years
until the sky grew so old
that it was strange to them. Because
the axis of the Earth is not now
as it was then.

This observatory at Karahunj required
planning, design, organization, mathematics and
astronomy.
Conventional archeology
teaches us that nine thousand years ago
there was no written language.
There was not even the wheel.

The Observatory at Karahunj, is a message.

In the desert, southeast of Istanbul
stands Gobekli Tepe.
Twelve thousand years ago;
three thousand years before the Karahunj
Observatory;
the final circle of the massive, ornately carved
stone pillars of Gobekli Tepe, already ancient
was abandoned by those who used it, and
then purposely buried in sand and rubble.
There are many more buried circles
much older, waiting to be uncovered
at Gobekli Tepe, beneath the sand.

Gobekli Tepe is a message that has been waiting
for 12,000 years to be noticed.

In Brittany, on the western coast of France
in eleven ancient rows almost two miles long;
stand the 2395 remaining stones of Carnac.
These stones weigh 50 to 350 tons each.

There were once 3000 massive stones at Carnac
arranged in rows as straight
as the columns of Roman legions
which would not arrive there for
another four thousand years.

Here is the math on tons:
It takes 10 to 20 men to move a

single

one ton

block of stone.

The wheel was not invented until 3500 BC
a thousand years after Carnac was built.
And that was in Mesopotamia, 2600 miles away.
It is said that the Carnac Stones were placed by
hunter-gatherers, fresh out of the stone age.

A three hundred fifty ton stone
requires seven thousand men
to move it.
A single stone.

And there were three thousand stones.

Moved by hunter-gatherers - fresh out of the stone age?

Carnac is another message.

No one was ever
buried in the Great Pyramid at Giza.
It was the tallest man-made structure on Earth,
for 3800 years, until the Eiffel Tower was completed
in Paris, in 1889.

The Pharaohs thought that they were gods.
With egos this big, if it were a tomb
someone would have used it.
No one was buried there – ever.

If it was not a tomb
what was it?

The stones are cut so precisely on every surface
that the average opening between the inner blocks
is only a half millimeter (1/50th of an inch).

The base of the pyramid covers 13 square acres
(think 10 football fields) and the entire area
is horizontal and flat
to within plus-or-minus
about half an inch.

The four sides of its base
each one, 785 feet long
have an average error
of only two and a quarter inch.

It's not a matter of the pharaoh ordering people
to build it or they would all be put to death.
The technology to build the Great Pyramid
did not (ostensibly) exist at the time.
The Egyptians needed iron to cut the stones, and
all they (officially) had was copper.

It's like a ruler today
ordering someone to build a time machine.
It's not possible, within the bounds
of our existing technology.

The Valley Temple at Giza, in Egypt
is constructed with hundreds of
blocks of stone that weigh 100 to 200 tons, each.
Many of them had to be put into place
by lifting them 40 feet
into the air.
(Do the math.)

The question is not so much "how" did they do this?
But "why" did they do this?

Why build with stones so huge
that they are nearly impossible to move.
Difficult even with 21st Century, heavy equipment?
Why not just use smaller stones?

The ancient Temple of Jupiter
in Baalbek, Lebanon, has foundation stones
weighing 800 to 1200 tons.

(Again, do the math. How many men would it take?)

These stones had to be moved 10 miles
from their quarry, then lifted 50 feet
into the air
to be put into place.
And their placement preceded
by some time, the Temple of Jupiter
which was built later, atop them.

The Great Pyramid
the Valley Temple, and
the Temple of Jupiter
are messages.

Paleontology tells us that man has walked the Earth
in some form or another
for more than 1,000,000 years.
Are we to believe
that he just sat around picking his nose
developing virtually nothing new, until 3500 BC?
And then, for some unknown reason
in the past five thousand years,
made it to the moon and onto YouTube?

Much of what is now dry land
was once under the ice.

Much of what was then dry land
is now under the sea.

Perhaps, all along
we've been digging for information
in the wrong place.

The Earth spins through space
like a bottle caught in a tidal whirlpool.
A bottle containing messages.
Messages containing secrets.

      --Graves 9/5/20

Ollantaytambo

In Peru, among the Andes
nine thousand feet above the Pacific Ocean
was built the ancient city
of Ollantaytambo.

Before the Inca
were the Urin Pacha.
Where they came from
we have no idea.
But they lived.
And they built "The Wall of the Six Monoliths"
in the city of Ollantaytambo.

According to authorities, the "Stone Age" ended
around 5,000 years ago, with the appearance
of bronze tools.
The earliest parts of Ollantaytambo
were built 12,000 years ago.
"The Wall of the Six Monoliths", it seems
was built earlier than that.

The Wall is composed of six
huge, red-granite stones
weighing more than fifty tons each
set together with such precision
with such uniformity, that a human hair
cannot pass between them.

And between these massive stones
are narrow, precisely engineered
vertical, stone shims,
placed between the stones
so that the wall is able
to ride out a major earthquake
and survive.

These "Stone Age" people brought these
50-ton stones here.
Up this mountain.
9,160 feet above sea level
from somewhere else.

Then they precisely carved, and set
these stones in the earth.

The ancient site at Ollantaytambo, and
the other walls built by these builders
are constructed largely of andesite.
A very hard rock.
Island chains are made of andesite:
the Aleutians. The crust of Mars.
In order to cut andesite
you need something harder than andesite.
There were no tools in the "Stone Age"
that were harder than andesite.

In the ancient walls of Ollantaytambo
(as opposed to the newer walls
which are different);
the stones are not set with mortar. They are

simply stacked
one
upon
the
other
like
a fieldstone fence in a meadow of grass.

But they have been bonded
into place, somehow
as though molded, one to another.

Stone Age technology?

It is not a question of how
so much; (though, really it is)
as it is a question of why?

And the answer is: "Because they could."

Stone Age technology?
Evidently.

It is not a question of man-hours.
Because from what we are taught
by authorities
the technology to do these things
did not exist.
Does not yet exist.
But the proof is there.
Formed from stone.

"Not possible."

A thing is only impossible, if it could not be.
Yet, having taken place - well
what does that say?

The Wall is there.
Go to Peru.
See for yourself.
Do the search: "Wall of the Six Monoliths."
You will find it.
You will find the impossibly quarried
impossibly set, impossibly designed stone wall
which has been standing
for more than 12,000 years.

But as you look; keep in mind
that these are only six of the stones.
There are more.

If you wanted to leave a message
that would last through time,
here is how you would do it:

Build something.
Put it somewhere where it would not be torn down.
Make it big enough to be noticed
and design it so that nature cannot destroy it.

And what exactly is this message?
"We were here?"

The trail through time is perhaps
not so straight nor clear as it is portrayed
by those who cannot think outside
the lessons that they have so rigidly, studiously
learned
from those who rigidly, studiously
learned them first.

It is interesting, the lengths to which
a person might go to explain something
which does not fall within the framework
of what they know;
in terms of that which they have been taught.
Rejecting contrary evidence.

That, however, is the route to
ignorance, demagoguery, intellectual abrogation

and perdition.

      --Graves 9/8/18

Glossary:

Inca: The **Inca Empire** was the largest empire in pre-Columbian America. The Inca Civilization arose from the highlands of Peru sometime in the early 13th century, and the last Inca stronghold was conquered by the Spanish in 1572.

Pre-Columbian: The pre-Columbian era incorporates the history prior to the landing of Columbus in the Americas and particularly refers to the time prior to the significant incursion of European influence on indigenous culture.

Red Granite: Granite is an igneous rock with a hardness of between 5 and 7 on the Mohs scale of mineral hardness.

Iron: A metallic element with a Mohs hardness rating of 4 compared to the hardness of a diamond which is 10 on the Mohs scale. Copper, one of the recorded first metals to be made into tools, has a hardness rating of between 2.5 and 3. Bronze has a Mohs hardness rating of 3.

Shim: A thin, often tapered or wedged piece of material

Andesite: An igneous, volcanic rock with a hardness rating of 7 on the Mohs scale.

Point of View: Escape Velocity

At first
the challenge is to open
your eyes
and see your nose

pressed hard against
the dark wooden floor.

An ant
an inch from your face
is crawling quickly
away, across the wide
6-inch expanse of floorboard.

Look upward
and the wall
stretches up, up to the metal doorknob
on the thick, massive
oak door; which slowly
swings open
wide to the outside air, and
the broad, green, grass-covered
front yard which stretches
all the way from the end of the porch
out to the edge of the road, which runs

for miles, alongside rolling
grassy fields, until it reaches the lake:
Twenty square miles of deep
wide water rippling away to
that place in the far distance where
hills begin; and run all the way out to the
base of the distant high mountains that rise
high into the
rapidly darkening sky that stretching
far, far out past the moon, through a place so

vast

that there are only stars
as distance-markers in a space so empty

so high,
so wide,
so deep,

so quiet

that its only visible points of light
measure the spaces
between them
in the number of years that it takes
their light to reach, and pass
and continue.

So quiet.

Go beyond that place where
there are no stars;
to the very outermost extent
of the universe, which
expands

in all directions

at the speed of
thought.

And from the edge of that place
so high
so vast

look around
and realize that you
are outside
of your head.

And be amazed
at what you see.

("Like the ride?"
asks the carnival barker,
grinning, and adjusting his hat.
"Try it again!")

      --Graves 10/16/20

Sailing (Song of the Daemons*)

The hull of my boat is painted blue.
We moor sometimes to clouds.
Eon to eon we've sailed out
on summer winds, into autumn
and back again 'cross tumultuous skies
riding the raging storms of winter
into the passionate arms of spring.

Our tides are the golden sunset
and the fiery red of dawn.
We ride the cool, black pre-dawn winds
soaring on broad remnants of darkness
between the ebb of moonlight and
the sparkling of the stars.

Sometimes, on a calm spring day
or blustery autumn afternoon
we'll lie-to off a cloud bank
and watch life unfold below.

You might have felt us watching.
Felt a presence where no presence was.

That was us
or maybe not.

You might have felt the unexpected
breath of air, one dead-calm day.

And known
without quite knowing
that it was us passing by.

The movement out the corner of your eye
that makes you turn your head

and see nothing but the crystal air
was us.

Or maybe not.

We course the currents below the storm
and above the raging sea.
It's we who send the dolphins out
to foundering ships

sometimes.

We spare the fleeing refugee.
We wake the pilot mid his flight.
We send the rains to quench the fire.
We cause the ticking bomb to fail.
We turn the tide when all seems lost

sometimes.

We tip the scales a bit, because
you strive when others might lose hope.

And as you do
we pause to intervene.
Sometimes.

                –Graves 11/6/20

*Daemon: noun, Daemons are good or benevolent nature spirits; beings of the same nature as both mortals and gods, similar to ghosts, spirit guides, forces of nature or the gods themselves (see Plato's Symposium), unlike the Judeo-Christian use of demon in a strictly malignant sense.

I used this term not because I was describing daemons, per se, but because it was the term that most closely described the hero-beings who are the subject of this piece.

Simplicity

When I gaze into
the deep universe
with closed eyes
I do not exist in
time and space
I simply am.

I feel the motion
of the dance of massive
stars in space.

I sense the flight of tides
on the Earth; pulling
heavily to another edge
of the sea.

I join in song
with deep
slow
sounds
made by the growth of
thousand-year-old trees.

I bathe in blinding coronal fire
and sense the throbbing
of the blazing sun.

I ride the currents that
carry glittering dust
between receding stars
at speeds approaching light.

When I fly in my dreams
I am not growing older.
I am not moving
through time.

I simply am.

                   -- Graves 11/13/20

NOTE: There are those who say that consciousness, or the soul, exists independent of the components of this universe; participating in it at will.
Glossary:

Coronal (from corona): A corona is a plasma atmosphere which surrounds the sun and other celestial bodies. It extends millions of miles into space. The sun's corona is much hotter (by a factor of nearly 200) than the visible surface of the sun, which averages around 5800 degrees Kelvin. The coronal temperature ranges from one to three million degrees Kelvin.

Spiderwebs and Evolution

Why do spiders all
make their webs exactly
the same way?

I mean, there is no
red-brick spider-school they go to
where they sit in rows and attend
design classes.
Right?

No instruction manual issued:
Some ancient, dusty tome passed
down through generations
on how to structure a web.

No seminar, workshop, website (sorry)
nor blog.

God? Whispering
secrets to each
individual spider?
I would think
that he/she/it has
better things to do.
No . . .
I don't think so.

How is it that they
all know how to build webs?
So that they ripple
in the breeze, just so;
like glistening, silken
banners of some alien civilization?
Or hold firm, like
cracks in a shattered
pane of air?

How is it that they know
how to cross the
staggering distances
to the opposite anchoring
point? How to string them above the
ground?
How to link together
each
strand, so that they
each
serve their appointed structural task?
So that they don't tangle
collapse, and wind up
a snarled, silken heap?

Instinct?

Instinct – I think – is the simple
stock answer for people
too stupid or too
cursory to admit that they have
no idea.

DNA?
Who/what programmed it?
Sounds a lot like "instinct."

Why do spiders
all make their webs
the same way?

Well, ALL spiders probably
don't make their webs
exactly the same way.

But a lot of them
a WHOLE lot of them
do.

I wonder why this is?

And evolution . . .

Life evolves.
But why?

Evolution posits
Life forms changing
(due to survival advantages) over
millions of generations so that
they can survive better.

It sounds reasonable.
But

the math doesn't
seem to work.

A change happens in one gecko.

A flash of mutation. And maybe
that gecko survives better.
And maybe he (or she)
doesn't get eaten by a bird
stepped on by an elephant
swallowed by a fox or smashed
by a falling branch.

One gecko.

And even if he does survive
it's only

one gecko

out of millions
(of the old-model gecko).

The gene pool it seems, would – by
mass of sheer inertia –
favor the old-model gecko.

It's like a crapshoot.
And eventually all crapshoots
crap out. By dint of numbers.
The house wins.
The "usual" prevails.

I'm not so much a "creationist"
necessarily

but it seems like Darwin missed a variable
or two
in the equation.

And it seems like
(since he'd already "done the math") that
"people" (as many people do) went along with it.
Because it sounded good, and they
didn't want to do the math.

So what is the answer?

I think the real answer is:
"Re-check the math."

Spiderwebs and evolution.

Tip of the iceberg.

        –Graves 6/6/15

Note: In case you were wondering: Geckos have the ability to run up walls, but it's not because their feet are sticky. Geckos have two billion, spatula-tipped filaments per square centimeter on their toe pads. Each of these filaments is only a hundred nanometers thick. This makes them so small that they interact at the molecular level with the surface on which the gecko walks, tapping into the low-level van der Waals forces generated by the fleeting positive and negative charges of molecules in the surface that the gecko is climbing. And their feet are constructed so that this gripping ability works in just one direction.

Crapshoot: "Craps" is a dice game in which the players make wagers on the outcome of the roll. Informally, the game of craps is sometimes called "shooting dice" hence: crapshoot. The game of craps is set up so that, while lucky players can win a significant amount of money; the odds involved in the game are such that the establishment sponsoring the game (the "house") always profits in the long run. To "crap out" is to lose. This generally happens when both dice being rolled, total a 2, 3 or 12.

The Dahlia

The sun in blazing splendor rose
and made its way into the sky.
And all beneath the blinding orb
turned down a dazzled eye.
From far below that fiery ball
which shines from out beyond.
Echoing the blazing sun
the dahlia responds

              --Graves 7/8/12

The Root of Strength

Complexity is a Siren's song, which
haunts the labyrinthine path.
It is the spawning seed
which births the lies that
hold the world in thrall.
Infinitely fragile constructs
susceptible to toppling by
any who simply look
and see.

For those who will not
the world ends just beyond
the edge of the familiar.
It ends at the whisper which
casts doubt upon the way that
they were instructed to believe.

For, beyond that point
is blindness. And
the terrifying void.

You fashion your potential;
your personal universe, so-to-speak
and your destiny
from that which you decide
to see and understand.

For that which you understand
you may control.

Or not.

As you choose.

In the simplicity
of understanding
you will find the root
of strength.

              –Graves 3/5/21

Visitor

It's always puzzled me just a little;
why it is that waterfalls flow
only in one direction?

Why not a nicely executed loop or two
on the way down?
Or a spiral like a woman's ringlet
dancing on her shoulder?

And why is it, the sky
must overarch the Earth;
so staunchly monochromatic
except for twice a day?

And why is it, the sun and moon
just travel a simple curve
across the wide, broad sky?
A figure-eight or for variety's sake
a curlicue, even a small one
might be nice.

All that space.
All that sky.

And why do clouds, horizon-bound, drift
silently, instead of being laced
with music, coaxed from the air, like a
moving bow across a violin?

Why is it?

This place might have more tourist appeal
with just a tweak
a minor adjustment
a helpful nudge here and there.

Other places have these things.
I see them yet in memories
at night while I'm asleep.

And why does time move only straight ahead
leaving memories as souvenirs?
It would be so convenient to have the option
of moving sideways through time
so one might sample other paths.

And why are solids always so damned solid?
It makes learning to rollerblade, problematic.
To say nothing of taking all of the fun out of
slamming a door on your finger.

And distance – why must it be so autocratic?
To hear your soft whisper
in my ear at night
from a thousand miles away would be
an exquisite experience.

And what if music
came in colors?
If ideas carried flavors
you could taste on the tip of your tongue?

I'm offering these points, simply
for your consideration as you
build this place.

I'm only a visitor here
stopping in, from time to time
to smell the breeze
and feed the ducks.

    --Graves 5/14/16

SOCIAL RESPONSIBILITY

America 2197

You are not what you once were. Nothing
is. Life changes. Life
evolves. Life
encompasses. Or life
dies.

Where once you lounged, cloaked
in alabaster privilege; steel
ribbons stretching edge to
edge, binding east to west; sleepless
fires in your massive coal forges spewing
forth your iron might:
You now sing

the tight, electric harmony.
Photons eclipse electrons.
Cloud surmounts earth.
Lines, long ago fallen before
the ubiquitous Net have been carried away
like pruned canes in a
vineyard now out of season.
Your roots have lengthened
and mingled, drawing life from the ends
of the spherical Earth.

You scan the far horizon with
Viking eyes; fiercely blue
fearing nothing.
The cold wind strews your flaming
Scottish hair and you smile
the knowing smile of one
certain to win all.

On the night air, your sweet Arabian lips call my
name
with cool aplomb and draw me close
murmuring tales of the Rub'al-Khali.
Of Dubai, before
the oil came
to your new home.

The sultry breeze whispers against
your smooth skin: Ebony silk
in the quiet morning of this new day. The cruel
uphill fight to attain, attain, attain
now so old as to be
legend. A curio
on a bracelet of charms.

Your voice dances in my ears
my sweet Parvati, and whets
all of my senses.
The gods of ancient Dwarka speak
through your fingers, and weave the future.
The ancient navigators of
Micronesia, now plot courses past
the stars with ease.
The sea was, after all
just practice.

The tango of the Argentine
speaks in your blood, and cries out
for the inevitable conquest.
Your breath quickens at the scent
of opportunity, for you are one
not without the fiercest of passions.
The view from the peaks of Aconcagua and
Chimborazo
king and queen of the Andes
has sharpened the acuity of vision
that you bring to your new home
to the point that the hawk - not the eagle - is jealous.
For you too now share the aerie.

You are as unstoppable
as the unkillable persistence
of your beautiful Russian forebears.
As transcendently enduring in the face
of adversity as the ancient monks
of the Tibetan high plateau. Of
the pilgrim looking toward Mount Kailash
from Idaho.

You are so much more than you were.
And so much less than you will be.
My love.
My America.

      –Graves 2/12/15

Notes:

1. Rub'al-Khali: The Rub' al Khali or Empty Quarter is the largest sand desert in the world, encompassing most of the southern third of the Arabian Peninsula. It includes most of Saudi Arabia and areas of Oman, the United Arab Emirates, and Yemen. The desert covers some 250,000 square miles.

2. Parvati: Parvati, also known as Gauri, is a Hindu goddess, nominally the second consort of Shiva, the Hindu god of destruction and rejuvenation. Generally considered a benevolent goddess, she also has wrathful incarnations such as Durga and Kali. She is the gentle aspect of Mahadevi, the Great Goddess, with all other goddesses being her incarnations or manifestations.

3. Dwarka: Dwarka is a city and a municipality of Jamnagar district in the Gujarat state in India. Also known as Dwarawati in Sanskrit literature, Dwarka is one of the seven most ancient cities in the country. The legendary city of Dwarka was the dwelling place of Lord Krishna.

4. Aconcagua: Aconcagua is the highest mountain in the Americas (22,837 feet). It is located in the Andes mountain range, in the province of Mendoza, Argentina. It is one of the Seven Summits.

5. Chimborazo: Chimborazo is the highest mountain in Ecuador (20,564 ft). While Chimborazo is not the highest mountain by elevation above sea level, its location along the equatorial bulge makes its summit the farthest point on the Earth's surface from the Earth's center.

6. Mount Kailash: A peak in the Transhimalaya range in Tibet. It is considered a sacred place in four religions: Bön, Buddhism, Hinduism and Jainism. Tibetan Buddhists call it "Kangri Rinpoche" meaning "Precious Snow Mountain". Bon texts give it many names: "Water's Flower", "Mountain of Sea Water", "Nine Stacked Swastika Mountain". For Hindus, it is the home of the mountain god Shiva and a symbol of his power symbol "Om"; for Jains it is where their first leader was enlightened; for Buddhists, it is the navel of the universe; and for adherents of Bon, it is the abode of the sky goddess Sipaimen.

Friendship

Your enemy is not:

Christian
Muslim
Jewish
Hindu
Buddhist
Scientologist
Shinto
Sikh

He is not:

Palestinian
Israeli
American
Russian
Chinese
Japanese
Iranian
Indian
Pakistani

There are differences between men
that make them interesting.
That give them something to talk about.

Your enemy is the specific man
who would use these differences
to breed distrust, and then
carefully
fan that distrust into hatred.

That man plants seeds that
he has carefully gathered from his own
hatred.
He is a man who knows
no peace except death.
For him, there is no sunny laughter of children, only
the sound of young recruits to his cause.
And his cause is death.

He dances like the matador, inflaming
the bull with deception
and pain, to the point
that it cannot
think.
It charges anything that moves.
He leads it to death.

Nothing more.
He knows that
there is no gain
at the end of his road.

There are differences between men.
That is what makes them interesting.
They share similar dreams.

This man dreams of
setting them at
each other's throats. He
is enemy to them all.

Children play in green fields
in the warm afternoon.
He watches from the tree line, hidden
among the weeds. Plotting
ways to turn them into creatures
of hate.

Every country
every religion
every race
has these men.

The war is: All
of us, against the few
of them.

All of us.

      –Graves 3/31/18

POET'S NOTE: I originally published this piece in 2012. In 2017 I received an email from Aoiri Obaigbo of Nigeria who had seen it.

He spoke of the violent tribal conflicts in the region and asked that I write a Nigerian version of this piece that addressed those tribal groups and so I added the names of the Igbo, Hausa, and Yoruba tribes for him. He said that he would mass-distribute the piece and that he felt that it would contribute to a reduction of violence in the region. was honored to have been able to do this.
—MG

Mother is Listening

Stop yourself from speaking
from writing, painting or the expression
of ideas that represent the truth
because it might offend someone
and you stop yourself
because of fear.

Don't call it something else.
Don't try and pretend that it's right.
Or nice.
Because it's not.

Fear is anathema.
It perverts the vision
and mutes the mind.
It wraps the artistic voice in cotton batting.
Ask Picasso about Guernica.
Ask Dylan about Hattie Carroll.
Ask Goya about the Revolución.
Ask them their opinion of the "politically correct."
Ask Mandella about the politics of South Africa or
Ghandi about the benefits of colonialism to the
indigenous.
Ask Socrates about the taste of hemlock.

Mute your voice because the truth
sounds offensive to some, and you break
the wings of the soaring bird.
And in that moment
you begin the dance of the death of the soul.

The surveillance culture is rife with
the iconic presence of "Big Brother."
The politically correct, fear
the disapproval of "Mother."

Honesty is born of equity.
Decency is born of courage.

Big Brother is watching.
Mother is listening.
Piss on 'em!

                –Graves 2/8/18

The Belly of the Beast

The old foundation crumbles.
Things once held dear, move beyond control.
The strings of puppets stretch far and away
into a darkness prowled by monsters.
Rules once dictated by reason, waver
and flux beyond familiar form.

The consumption of innocence
proceeds unchecked. A harmony
of dissonance in a fiendishly
scripted meta-plan, too insidious
to be given credence by
gentle people
blindly singing
hopeful hymns
of redemption.

Clarity of insight is roundly cast as paranoia
by gnomes with hidden intent.
The bugle call of the watch is disregarded.
Its message rejected for "lack of proper form."

Controllers pivot and spin like the matador
in the Plaza de Toros, sowing seeds
of docility fertilized by fear
ignoring truth: Caring only
for believability in
the evening-news cycle.

The blood-hungry crowd
cheers the cruelty of the game.
Their voices: Orchestrated instruments in a
symphony spawned of influence and violence.
The maddened bull charges at
the swirling cape
connecting with nothing, save death.

Poison hides in the communion-wafer
doled out in false generosity to the indolent.
The lights of the theater have been
carefully set, and focused on
the bare boards of the stage.
Specters dance beyond the edges
of the light to ceremonial music of
the profane transubstantiation. Waiting to
feast on dying souls.

Truth is neither penurious nor kind.
It is merely truth.
It does not pause in pursuit to gather flowers
on a spring morning.
Nor change in the face of malice.
It makes no excuses for the unpleasant.
It does not mask the anomaly.
Truth sees with hard eyes which
brook neither obfuscation nor
fashionably convenient illusion. The choice
that is offered is:
Conform to it or be cast aside.

At the seeming end – when
all is shaken, and truth lies in bright
sharp shards upon the ground. When
integrity serves as the lone rallying point
a solitary island in that darkest sea;
take up the shining, razor shards of truth, and slice
and slice again, your way out
from the Belly of the Beast.

Those whose intention was never
to live in the light will hate you
even as you are saving them.
You must change the world
from where you stand.
And the light shining into the darkness within
will be seen by others and will bring them together
one by one.

And in the brilliance of the light
those who care to see
will change the world.

                    –Graves 3/30/18

Vengeance '*lex talionis*' (For the suicide bombers)

The path of vengeance is paved
in blind, smoldering hatred.
A traveled road, lined with damned souls
set to fall like dominoes, one against the other.
It does not end
until all lie writhing in the dust.

A hot, dry wind is all that remains
at the end of this path. A wind
which carries no joy
no satisfaction.

"But the law says: 'An eye for an eye!'
It is only just!"

No.
It is not.

"An eye for an eye" is a crime committed by
translators
in thrall to those thirsting for blood and
for self-serving tumult; translating
for the convenience of those who live to wage death.

The proper reading should be:
"For an eye that is taken, an eye should be replaced."

An eye for an eye.

A life for a life is a far more complex proposition.
It is not true that death, as a solution
is never warranted. But vengeance
begets naught but vengeance.
A repetition of itself, as a round sung
in an unholy song; voiced
in an eternally minor chord.

No life. No happiness.

The appearance of satisfaction, real only to he
whose gaze is fixedly inward. . . .
He who dances alone in his murderous - "I told you
so" - existence.
He is a mote of dust in a barren, soulless
empty land which bears no solace.

You would justify your pain
by adding to the universe, more pain?
You ignorant, self-righteously arrogant child!

You would justify your existence by the death of those
into whose eyes you've never looked!

Justice is a more difficult job.
It is not as easy as killing.
Violence is only done where fear is first present.
Vengeance begets only death and vengeance.
It does not balance the scale.

But you knew that from the beginning
and did not care; bearing the rage-fueled seed

which is nurtured only by the compulsion to inflict pain.

If you want true justice:
Get those who created your pain
to understand, and face without denying, the
horror of their acts; and then to make
effective and acceptable amends.
By their own choice.
By their own hand.

    –Graves 1/27/18

Watch Me

In your darkest night
when they've beaten you down
and told you that you will not rise.
Raise your head and say to them:

"Watch me."

And when they've said
what's yours is theirs
and you will never take it back.
Match their gaze with yours
and tell them:

"Watch me."

And when by guile
they block your path
and tell you, you'll not reach your dreams
I will expect to hear you say:

"Just watch me."

And you will stand, you will persist
and you will overcome, I know.
'Cause I have heard you say before:

"Watch me."

--Graves 11/18/15

The Vengeance of Angels

The bright morning belies the peace.
Grasses bend and spin in the fragrant air
on the walk to the sea.
The glory of the morning sun stains
my eyes, hiding with bright fire
the stones in the path.

Any turns – regardless of direction – that form
the road to attainment of the holiest
of causes are justified;
some say.

Malevolence lurks beneath the shimmering
surface of flowing words.
Beneath the surface of the water
a shark waits, hoping
for the smell of blood.

War engenders only hate.
Peace is relative.
In the vengeance of angels, lies
the pathway to hell.

–Graves 2/13/14

A Few Words on the Study of Philosophy

Educating a student by requiring that they simply memorize and recite data is like teaching an artist to paint using stencils. It makes it easy to teach painting, but it misses the the point of the exercise.

Teaching a subject while ignoring its philosophical implications and consequences, is like teaching writing or poetry by emphasizing grammatical or poetic form while glossing over the definitions of the words used in the piece. It is like teaching a student to paint scenes from life without teaching him the use of perspective. It produces an odd-looking product, lacking any sense of depth at best.

What if a society knew that murder was "bad," but didn't understand why it was "bad"? I'm not referring to the various religious mandates forbidding murder, but to the actual understanding of the ramifications of taking a life: The pain and destruction caused to the family and friends of the murdered. The damage to the groups and organizations in which the murdered person participated. The damage to the business at which the murdered person was employed. The direct consequences to the murderer: Not just prison or death, though that threat can be a deterrent; but the extreme metaphysical destruction which the act of murder wreaks on the well-being of the murderer? Would it change the number of murders that take place? I think that it would.

If the subject of ethics was understood to concern itself with rationality directed toward optimum survival in all areas of one's life; what might happen to the justice system when a practical understanding of the subject was widely known and practiced in a society? Would it put some attorneys out of business? I expect that it would. Might the general population look differently on the "win in the courts at any cost -- guilty or not" practices of many attorneys? I expect that it would.

How might it affect the results of an election in a democracy or a republic if the majority of the electorate understood the actual economic, political and ethical consequences of electing a particular candidate, rather than allowing themselves to be seduced by juicy-sounding, hollow campaign promises? Might this result in a self-correcting political system which then resulted in a leaner, better-balanced, more equitable government?

What if the majority of citizens in a country understood both the ethical and the economic consequences to that country, of allowing financial institutions to sell sub-prime home mortgages to tens of millions of people who did not qualify for them, as happened in the United States a relatively short time ago? Would perpetrators go to jail for this, or would they continue to collect massive bonuses? I'll leave the answer to you. But it wouldn't be bonuses. These are examples of conditions which might result if the majority of a population understood the subject of Applied Philosophy.

Prior to science, prior to art, prior to technology, prior to advances in any field: There is philosophy.

Philosophy consists, broadly, of two parts: "theoretical" and "applied". Theoretical Philosophy is arguably the aspect of the field that most people think of when they think of "philosophy." It involves musing, speculation, conjecture and extrapolation of whatever nature, regardless of any bearing that it may have on actual existence. And it may have significant bearing – or it may not.

The field of Applied Philosophy involves taking the conjecture, the vision, the product of reason, and integrating its application into the interactions of humanity in order to change conditions.

A balanced, accurate study of philosophy, effectively undertaken -- from Marx to Rand, from Nietzsche to Plato, from Kant to Hubbard, from Jefferson to Lao Tzu, from Rene Descartes to Siddhartha Gautama and many others, endows a perspective from which to assess problems and circumstances and arrive at sane conclusions. It equips a person to reason.

In general, our education system does not equip students with the ability to understand, assess and address points like those above; except from an autocratic "it is law and you must obey!", point of view. The system -- for the most part -- teaches students to paint with stencils. It creates a cursory, mass-produced "product" in the area most important to the continuance of a culture -- its future citizens. It takes the easy route and misses a major purpose of the exercise.

Those whose goal it is to keep the human soul enslaved, work to portray the philosopher -- the free thinker -- as a worthless freeloader. The philosopher, however, embodies the driving, creative force which goes out beyond the edge of that which is known, and shapes the future by first conceiving it, and then by bringing that concept back, to be put into effect.

Any of those men and women whom we consider great in a culture, had to first conceive of the breakthrough(s) for which they are responsible; and then think their way through problems, to arrive at solutions, and then to implement those solutions. In doing that, they were practicing Applied Philosophy.

Will the study of philosophy guarantee greatness? Nope. But I challenge you to name a single person whose accomplishments produced any enduring value to a culture, who did not have a solid familiarity with some aspect of the subject.

Our politicians would be better at their jobs if they had studied, understood and applied more of it. They would deal more responsibly in terms of rational consequences. Our Statesmen are what they are, because they have done this.   --Graves 5/6/16

A Red Horse in a Fallow Field

A red horse stands in a fallow field.
In the morning air
I can hear the Union cannons booming
a mile away. Maybe less.

It all seemed so noble once;
the fife, the drum
the marching off to war.
To defend the ones I love.
To make them proud.
To turn the tide of death away.

A quiet farm.
A grassy knoll.
And you, waiting for my return.
When I return. Now
if I return.

A red horse stands in a fallow field.
The sounds of death are no longer
in the distance.
They are personal.
I hear the sounds from bayonets.
The whine of bullets in the air.
The repeating boom of the Henry rifle.
The sound of the Gatling gun.
My friends are dying.
Yet, I still live.
For how long?
I think of you, waiting
for me.

I see that red horse standing in a field
not half a mile away.
I see blue-clad prisoners of war
who shall never see their homes.
Who left to fight.
To turn the tide of death away
from friends
and those they love.

The morning mist that hangs above the field
is now the lingering smoke of guns; fallen silent
among the fallen.
And no one with time
to bury all of them.
I watch the ravens begin their timeless chore.
We fall back into the trees.

A red horse stands in a fallow field.
The rolling hills.
The quiet glen.
Thoughts of you, beside the stream.
Another place. Another day.

Not so noble now, this business.
My one desire is to live through it
and return home.
And in the field, there stands a red horse.

     --Graves 2/19/16

Notes:

It was while I was driving through Kentucky in March 2013 on a trip to the East Coast that this haunting poem came to me, as an almost complete communication. I was looking at the lush, green countryside rolling past the car window, and in the distance, standing alone in a field, I saw a red horse. And suddenly the piece arrived. It was as though I was remembering it, along with its accompanying emotions, rather than writing it. At that point it became my duty to put the piece to paper and to make sure that it was seen. To me, these are the thoughts of a Confederate soldier as the advantage of war turned to the side of the Union and as the inevitable came into sight.

During the American Civil War (1861 – 1865) more than 360,000 Union troops - both Black and White -- died in the effort to abolish slavery in the United States. More than 260,000 Confederate troops also died in that conflict. (ref. http://www.historynet.com/civil-war-casualties)

Henry rifle: The original Henry repeating rifle was patented in 1860 and fired up to 17 shots before needing to be reloaded. Except for relatively rare exceptions, it was employed by Union forces. Most rifles of the time were rifled muskets which fired a single shot, after which they had to be reloaded – a relatively slow process. There were an estimated 12,000 Henry repeating rifles manufactured during the time of the American Civil War. A relatively small number; but their increased firepower made them arguably a deciding factor in more than one battle.

Gatling gun: The Gatling gun is one of the best-known early rapid-fire weapons and a forerunner of the modern machine gun. Invented by Richard Gatling in 1861, it is known for its use by Union forces during the American Civil War. This was the first time it was employed in combat.

All Lives Matter

I believe that All Lives Matter.
Not just Black lives or White lives
or Brown lives or Yellow lives
or Red lives.

Mankind is a homogenous mass.
And most of us like it that way.
Our differences give us something
to discuss and to reflect upon.
A conglomeration of colors,
features and ideas. Variety
beyond imagining.

I believe that All Lives Matter
not just one faction or another
and I believe that this is the
creed that we should strive to attain.
Not some self-serving political
activity that mostly benefits its
leadership by pitting one pie-slice
of humanity against another.
That's an old song sung in a
minor key, time after time
in history by singers
both religious and political.

If you want to paint me
racist (as some have – go figure)
for believing that All Lives Matter
then I say "Go fuck yourself!"
And take your perverted
definition with you.

Your purpose in using the word "racist"
is not to identify a morally
reprehensible condition, but to bend
others to your will, who are
either intellectually too
slow or morally too submissive
to see the incongruity in its use.

By definition, it is racist
to hold one pie-slice
of humanity inferior
to another by virtue of
nothing more than
genetic markers.
That's what the word means.

The only people who respond with
guilt to your fraudulently-flung epithet
are those good people who
in their hearts understand that
true racism is an evil trait and
who think that your use of the term
comes from honest misunderstanding, not
from manipulation. Actual racists
are too blind, too callous
and too intellectually in-bred
to either see the truth
or to care about your opinion.

I've seen people or color (any color)
bubbling with as much
self-righteous hate
as some white people.
I've also met both
who I am proud to call family.

I've met people, who self-servingly believe
that it makes perfect sense for
them to receive compensation for
wrongs which were committed
against others, long dead, by
others also long dead, and
to receive charity-as-amends
from people who did not
commit those wrongs. Free money.
This is truly the very, very long con.
I've met others who worked
diligently; who took handouts from none
and who achieved greatness.

I've met women who believe
that males are destructive
by nature, being hormonally
irretrievably committed to that path.
Women wallowing in their own
self-serving, bitter blindness, as though
goodness and evil were somehow
rooted in gender. I've seen men -
degraded, insecure and evil -
who believed that they were entitled
to treat women as little more than property.
And I've met those of both genders
who were exemplary, compassionate
human beings.

I've seen politicians, who
would sell every individual
that they represent into economic
slavery while lining their
pockets with power and
with gold taken from
those people, all the while gently
reassuring them that this slavery
is for their own good.
And I've seen Statespeople who
worked selflessly, tirelessly
to the benefit of their
constituents. Accomplishing
good, against staggering odds.

You've heard it said that
there are no passengers
on Planet Earth.
We are all crew.
All Lives Matter.

I've seen religious figureheads, who
manipulate the truth to create
minions bound blindly
to them by their assertion
that they are the only conduit
to a higher power.
In that final court of appeals
they will be the most harshly judged
for their misappropriation of
spiritual funds.
And I have seen those spiritual
leaders with the ability
to genuinely set mankind free.

"There are no passengers
on Planet Earth.
We are all crew,"
None are inconsequential.
Learn this
or lose your way.

– Graves 6/27/21

America: The Election Year

Since its long-odds beginning, America
has danced beneath
the suspended, gleaming edge; tempting
the razor-sharp blade of fate to slide. Pivoting
one way and the other around
the axis of potential -- constantly
risking its release. Maintaining
its touch-and-go balance
on a fulcrum of finality. Commitment
or betrayal deciding
the ultimate condition.
On one side, the sweet kiss of freedom.
On the other, the looming abyss lined with
roads traveled by those less
fortunate, into lands far
more oppressive and wanting -- yet attractive to some
by force of visceral, ugly habit.

Balance requires attention and responsibility.
The plummet, none.

Balance requires action and adjustment.
The plummet, none.

Balance requires judgment and precision.
The plummet, none.

It is a precarious place that we occupy. Dreams and
practicality.

Freedom and control.
Truth and lies.

America is a trust.

I weary of your disregard for this.

I am growing very tired of specious
protestations, posturing and
bombast.
I am tired of sound bite
"explanations": Obfuscation, laced with
feigned sincerity.
The engineered attempt to
fill emptiness
by verbal sleight of hand.

And I'm really tired
of Socialist rhetoric.

I am tired of having: ". . . the
best politicians money can buy."
I am tired of "the party platform."
I am tired of the disrespect
for my intelligence.

This was not in the design of
how America works. This is how
you work America.
And it offends me.

Your implication of ethical
behavior is made all the more
tenuous by your fatuous invocation
of precedent.
It reeks of disingenuity."

                --Graves 9/12/22

Bricks

Believers scare me.

Believers kill people "just because" and
justify it with "they're different."
Two words.

Obliteration of human commonality, in
two words. Like squishing
a bug.

From one's first instant, until
the end; there is this choice:
One can Believe, or
one can understand.

Understanding is the dance
of the expanding mind. Belief
is the blind, determined
fruit of dictates, planted
in stony, shallow soil.

Nothing is understood without perceiving.
Blindness serves only the one who blinds
and his acolytes.

Understanding brings freedom to move
perhaps with ease
perhaps at cost. It is the dance.
Belief is the goose-step.

Blind Belief is a brick baked hard
in the raging fires
of authoritarianism, which demands
adherence and brooks no variance.
Obedience without question is
the mortar which holds
bricks
tightly in
prescribed
formation.

And some prefer that way of life.
I don't.
Some like the ease of life
that comes with never
having to find
the new answer. Bricks

can be anchors in turbulent times.
But they can drag you beneath the surface
of the deep water and pin you there until
you no longer breathe.

From the first instant, until
the end
there is the choice:

One can Believe
or one can
understand.

Personally, I continue to try and build windows
in empty space.
And then to open them
and climb out.

                –Graves 5/2/20

Circumstance

Circumstances slide against each other
forming situations.
Because that's what circumstances do.
Not entirely unlike tectonic plates
in their action and consequences.

They form ripples, building fluid waves
of opportunity
or condemnation
for being on the right or
the left side of the tide
of general assessment.

In such circumstantial times, the risk is being
burned in the auto-da-fe for seeing
too clearly the State
of the Emperor's clothes, and speaking.
Or for hearing and trying to rescue
the holy songs, drowning in the roar of the crowd.

For heresy or sainthood are determined
chiefly by the mood of the moment. The direction
of the tide. The alignment of circumstance.

Many saints, conveniently presented in witches'
clothing
have roasted in the pyre that was lit too soon
so as to hide their holiness;
simply because they were feared.

But what of it?

It happens to us all
I guess
from time to time.

You scare the wrong little people
– the minnows living in shallows, waiting
to be eaten by something –
whose job is not truth, but sales

and they begin gathering wood
and gasoline for the fire
in the service of agenda.

                      –Graves 8/21/15

Glossary:

Auto-da-fe: (noun) An auto-da-fé was the ritual of public penance of condemned heretics that took place when the Spanish Inquisition or the Portuguese Inquisition had decided their punishment, followed by the execution by the civil authorities of the sentences imposed. Both auto de fe in medieval Spanish and auto da fé in Portuguese mean "act of faith."

The most extreme punishment imposed on those convicted was execution by burning. As the execution was more memorable than the penance which preceded it, in popular use the term auto-da-fé came to mean the punishment rather than the penance.

"The Emperor's New Clothes": Is a short story by Hans Christian Andersen about two weavers who promise an Emperor a new suit of clothes that is invisible to those unfit for their positions, stupid, or incompetent. When the Emperor parades before his subjects in his new clothes, a child cries out, "But he isn't wearing anything at all!" It has been translated into more than a hundred languages.

Detergent

Everything
you see on TV is:
Written
Scripted
Produced
Acted
Directed
Edited
Sponsored.

Everything.

At best it is a scripted interpretation
of truth. Not truth itself. At worst it is a
manipulated depiction following
a larger agenda.

Perhaps you should be
a little less concerned
with who is listening
to your phone conversations
-- important as this is --
and be more interested in discerning
the type of detergent they have been using
on your brain.

                      --Graves 4/11/20

Don't

They want us to tire.
They want us to forget, thinking

that the American public is
too shallow, too weak to persist
in its beliefs past a news cycle

or two.
They want us, through apathy to
grow tired and "move on."
They want us weakened and
malleable so that they can
while not representing us
prevail and rule. And exercise
power.

They want us to grant – tacitly
the agreement that what they
do is somehow decent and "right."

Regardless of its purpose or
ethical grounds.
They want us to agree and
to follow them.
They want us to give up.

Don't.

                              --Graves 4/23/21

God: Getting Bored . . .

"I've watched over you
since before you crawled
in the dirt.

Babysitting
after long enough
becomes tedious.

I catch myself thinking that
this
should not be the full-time occupation
of an immortal, sentient being.

I love you

but

I am getting tired of
always having to

follow

the

money

like dirty footprints

across the kitchen floor

to find out what
you're up to.

You buy guns
when you should be
learning.

You breed diseases for killing
when you should be
helping the hungry child.

You choke the air, when
you should be playing.

You poison the seas, when
you should be saving
your future.

You are old enough, now
to wage
the final
war.

There are few --
too few --

who shine brightly enough to
make my job
interesting, at all.

I am

this!

close!

to kicking you

out of the house!

And if you don't survive... well
there are other

canvases to paint.

There are other places
to populate with flowers
and sentience.

I am not your excuse to kill.
I am not your reason to suppress.
I am not your justification for hatred.
I am not your excuse for theft.
I am not your right to wreak havoc.

It

does

not

MATTER! which
of my names
you invoke.

I am getting TIRED of
babysitting.

Despite what you think
my patience is NOT eternal. And
saying that it is
does NOT!
make it so.

Carelessly electing me
to clean up
your mess

leaving it to me
to pull your disingenuous hand
back from the fire
yet again

will no longer do.

Maybe now is the time
for me to say
'Fix it yourself.'

You need to clean up your room."

     --Graves 12/5/15

How to Cook a Frog

First, catch a frog.
Then put him in a nice
pot of water.
Make sure it's comfortable
so that he's lulled into
a false sense of security.
Then turn the heat up, just
a bit. Still comfortable. Then,
Turn the heat up a little more.
At some point he may object
to the heat, but not enough
to do anything about it.
Keep turning up the heat until
the water is hot enough to cook
the frog.
Then you can eat him.

Stupid frog.

Sound familiar?

                    ---Graves 11/20/22

In killing me . . .

For each body lying dead
upon the bloodied field
an entire path through time
lies now bereft.

Parents grieve.
Children weep in the lonely nights.
Companions mourn.

Lovers wail in anguish
bound by knotted sheets
no longer warm.
Spring is smothered by winter's shroud.

The kind word never comes.
The outstretched hand is never offered.
Night runs an empty, hollow course.

No joy remains.

In killing me, you steal a share of life
from everyone that I have known.
Everyone I would have known.
All who would have read my works or
heard my voice.

In killing me, you kill
that part of yourself, which
in the killing, you deny.   --Graves 7/31/20

Maniac (for Syria)

The morning is soft and
wet with stained
dew among the fallen.

The black birds are circling below
the clouds
awaiting the feast.

You have already forgotten the day
and plot the night; hungry
for justification.

The innocent impaled.
The defenders left rotting;
turning the field fecund for your hollow posturing.

We marched on them
caught up in the call. Our pay laced
with the promise of ribbons. But

there is no honor in killing
children. No glory in the death of
civilians waiting simply for the cessation of noise.

The small white dog walks
the fields and digs
his nose into the fresh morning earth. And

the truth now fills us
who are left, with shame. Though remorse
in excess, is paid with death.

We raise our voices, and
the new arrivals focus hard on the horizon. Seeing
fevered visions of heroics.

Their heads high with
determination. Imagined validity, in
the seamless glory of an unchallenged purpose.

Their step springs with green.
The spring, to them is a time for games.
And so it is.

For they have not yet seen death.
Nor smelled the blood that fouls
the roses of delusion.

You expect us to run
into the guns for you.

I will not run
into the guns for you.

+++++++++++++++++++++++–Graves 4/28/16

Note:

Homs: A city in western Syria, about 100 miles north of Damascus. It is also the central link between the interior cities and the Mediterranean coast.

Prior to the civil war, Homs was a major industrial center, with a population of more than 650,000. Its population reflects Syria's general religious diversity, composed mostly of Arabic-speaking Sunni Muslims and Alawite and Christian minorities. The **Siege of Homs** was a military confrontation between the Syrian military and the Syrian opposition in the city of Homs as part of the Syrian Civil War. The siege lasted three years from May 2011 to May 2014 and resulted in an opposition withdrawal from the city.

Nationwide anti-government protests began in March 2011, and clashes between security forces and protestors in Homs intensified in April. In May 2011, the Syrian military conducted a crackdown against anti-government protesters, some of whom were armed and fired on security forces. Unlike previous crackdowns conducted elsewhere in Syria, the operation in Homs failed to quell the unrest. The city was also unique for its relatively high level of sectarian violence. As soldiers defected and protesters took up arms, the situation evolved into prolonged street fighting between security forces and insurgents, who gained ground and the control of several quarters of the city.

By 14 January 2014, the government was in control of Homs except for the Old City. The Syrian army's artillery shelling and warplane bombing has left much of the city completely destroyed and thousands dead.

In May 2014, rebel forces withdrew from all areas in Homs, as per the truce.

On Social Media

Four and a half billion of us.
Connected.
Solitude and communication
our commonality.
Interaction in an empty room.

I go outside and smell the sweet
scent of redwoods, sweating
in the summer sun.
I touch the coarse earth.
I hear the baby raccoons, playing
on my back deck
in the summer night. Knowing

that I will return to
that connectivity, over which
I have most control and
arguably, least prediction.

A universe shaped
by a myriad of potential
conversation. By a dearth of
physical interaction. Composed
of a virtual malestrom of
personality, opinions, ideas, and emotions.

Its components: The loftiest among us, and
the most debase. The finest and the most coarse.

I see you.

I wish, sometimes
that I could see you.

> --Graves 7/20/18

Poseurs

In thrall to the god of baseless awe
they glitter in the light.
Not themselves radiant, but an
imitation of radiance.
Theft by reflection.
Tinsel without depth.
An image of accomplishment, rooted
in pretense.

Attention from those
who know no better than
to senselessly dart at shiny lights
is their sought reward.

All is for show.

Adorned like minor Emperors, they
strut in their new clothes.
Carefully tailored garb
stitched with threads of
folly, dyed in hues of
pretentious affectation.
Naked in front of
all who can see.

They posture -- and they believe
that this is accomplishment;
that paraded pretense is sufficient.
Poseurs, with no further goal than
to appear in the light as genuine.
For long enough to impress.
For long enough to cash in.

To appear as -- rather than to be.

It has come then, to this:
The image of importance, has
now the capacity to hold sway.
Appearance alone, sufficient
to evoke respect, requiring
no proof of capability -- of value.
Just posturing and pretense.

Their followers, naught but
brainwashed sheep.
Bereft of substance.

The wolves leer.

                    --Graves 10/18/20

Superhuman Monkeys (Song Lyrics)

I was waiting on the corner
when the light began to dawn.
It shocked me into realizing
how long I'd been gone.

There were monkeys running everywhere.
Monkeys on the street.
Everywhere I looked
I saw dancing monkey feet.

They were speaking ancient languages
so serious and vain.
I'd been down this road before
and thought, "Oh, here we go again..."

They're all superhuman monkeys...
Yeah, superhuman monkeys...
They're all superhuman monkeys
and they all seem to know my name.

They're pushin' pills to make you happy
after telling you you're sad.
Pills they say will cure you
of things you never had.

Pills that will distill you.
Pills that make you itch
Pills that just might kill you
while you're making them all rich.

They're all superhuman monkeys...
Yeah, superhuman monkeys...
They're all superhuman monkeys
and they all seem to know my name.

They're writing checks like it's a favor.
Free money for your dreams.
But all this cash they're handing out
is never what it seems.

At first it seems so wonderful; but
the reason is obscene
Their only role for you is as
a slave to the machine.

They're all superhuman monkeys...
Yeah, superhuman monkeys...
They're all superhuman monkeys
and they all seem to know my name.

They're lookin' flashy and attentive
linin' up to be inventive.
Your soul is their incentive
and it's never like it seems.

They'll dump you in a minute.
put the bottle down and spin it.
For someone else who's in it
with more glitter and more gleam.

They're just superhuman monkeys...
Yeah, superhuman monkeys...

They're all superhuman monkeys
and they all seem to know my name.

They're workin' hard to cover up the fact
they're only silly monkeys.
Like they're actually important, but
they're just somebody's flunkies.

They're superficial whiners and
they don't have any class.
They should take all of their whining noise
and blow it out their ass.

They're just superhuman monkeys...
Yeah, superhuman monkeys...
They're all superhuman monkeys
And they're never gonna guess my game.

                --Graves 12/8/16

Tahrir Square -- The Beginning -- The (more) complete version -- by Michael Graves and Eva Mihalik

A new day was dawning, the sun rising fast.
A new world was making its break with the past.
In the city of Cairo, new dreams were about;
new dreams that would usher the old regime out.

It started with messages spread 'cross the 'net
to brothers and sisters, to come and help set
the road to the future in another direction;
one that would lead to Mubarak's ejection.

The message was spread like the sun 'cross the land:
"Come down to Tahrir; come take a stand.
We'll meet in the square, and our voices will range.
In the square we will meet, and our future we'll change."

The dreams that had kindled these women and men
were to bring all Egyptians together, and then
together to take their fine country away
from the 30-year dictatorship that held sway.

They came from afar, they came from nearby
They came and they vowed that these dreams would not die
They stood fast as one and with voices so clear
said the wrongs of Mubarak will all stop here.

They stood through the night, they stood through the sun
They stood through the tear gas, they stood as one
They stood and continued their bold demonstration, and together they peacefully changed a whole nation.

In the fresh mists of morning, five hundred years free
The new eyes of Egypt will look and will see
That the ghosts of those heroes are still standing there with heads held high, in Tahrir Square.

--Graves 3/17/11

NOTE: The relatively bloodless overthrow of a repressive regime by the Egyptian people which started on 25 Jan 2011, may come to be known as one of the the most significant political events of this century. It came to the attention of the world in Tahrir (Liberation) Square.

The following is a series of letters from Eva Mihalik, who was there and talks about what she saw, in her own words.

Poet's Note: My friend Eva Mihalik passed away in mid-July 2013 as a result of a sudden illness. She will be missed. She is one of the good ones.

Eva Mihalik February 26 at 11:20am Report

Happily. I have 4 albums on Facebook: Cairo, 28.1.11, 30.1.11, 1-2.2.11 and 18.2.11. The first day I went out I went with a friend and I was very scared at the beginning but after a short while it changed and I just wanted to be with the protesters. We were near Tahrir but all streets were effectively blocked and it was so heroic that the crowd gathered again and again after every tear gas attack and tried again to get through. And what I liked very much that the tone was quite high and the people with running eyes and nose still could pay attention to help each other. Someone gave me a piece of onion what is good to neutralize the effect of tear gas. From the windows water bottles were thrown to the people down. They were giving water, tissues to each other. Other nice thing I saw another place where there were clashes with the police forces, that some women with a toddler was caught in a fenced park and could not get out, because the other side was the tear gas attack and here the gate was padlocked. And the police guy broke up a stone and broke the padlock off. And I saw later (tear gas everywhere) a man crossing the road and a young man was running to him with tissue. Somehow this all thing made people friends, you sat on a bus these days or in a restaurant and people quickly were in conversations. One occasion a man paid my fare on the bus, as he found out I was on my way to Tahrir. The other day I went out the army was out, but they were not like the police. There was even a soldier carried on shoulders among the protesters. And a new slogan appeared: the people and the army is one. I saw that someone was giving out oranges for the people in Tahrir and the general tone was quite cheerful but determined. And the people desperately wanted to be heard. They pushed their placards to your camera. I saw a dumb guy with a placard trying to shout and be heard. Then I next time I spent the whole day and night at Tahrir. And again, bread etc was disbursed (as far as I know individuals brought these things out of solidarity.) and the cleaning solved by volunteers. You could feel the people start to own the place and the country and the responsibility grew accordingly. And sweet thing was that people just shared their bread, water, fruit with me. One man lent his coat for me for the whole night. A stranger. We were waiting for Mubarak speech with big hope but he was just bullshitting and obviously did not want to leave. There was an immediate reaction of shouting their things again: leave, leave. The night was freezing, the floor hard but the mood was good, little fires lit for a bit of warm. And the next day there was the worst part with the pro Mubarak attackers, who injured and killed people. I was not there. Watched on the TV. But after that I wanted to go out again, could not help but feeling solidarity, and trust that no stray rock or bullet would hit me. But the streets were scary and people looked at me not as before. Before the Egyptians were the most friendly and helpful, but this day not. Later I heard that there were some announcements in the local media that the problem was caused by foreign agents. Also order was to prevent press to record the events. Lot of foreigners were arrested that day but locals too. Then I did not go out till 18 February to celebrate. I think this is my experience in a nutshell. Generally I felt it beautiful, the protesters were so heroic but kind too. I don't know how protests are in other places, it was beautiful here. Not the behavior of their attackers of course. I hope it helps. :-) Eva

Eva Mihalik, February 27 at 4:24am Report

If you don't mind I will add to you a few more data about what these people were up against. To add to the picture in this country crime is almost nonexistent. I could leave my door open regularly without anything missing. Cell phone forgotten in taxi gotten back, you can leave your bag with the laptop you just used on the train and go to the bathroom, give your phone to the first stranger if you don't know here you are to explain it to your friend who is to meet you, throw your wallet on a chair and turn your back to it in a shoe shop etc. And surprisingly huge police force existing compared to it. And an enormous number of secret police on the top of it. First of all it was common knowledge that anybody openly opposing the rule could end up in jail, tortured. At the beginning of the protest the people had to face the police brutality. Also the communication black-out. Then the police disappeared and criminals from jails freed and armed looters were roaming the country. It's an odd coincidence to say the least. So the people had to worry and organize defense for their family and property. Meanwhile the banks were closed, so the

people could not have access to their due salary and the shelves of the grocery shops emptying and the prices of food increasing. And there was the threatening presence of the army. I think the worst was the so called pro Mubarak protesters sudden appearance and brutality after all the previous attempts to beat down the uprising failed. Also appointing outside sources for the problems by the official medias.
After asking some of my friends it seems the majority of Egyptians prefer poetry with rhymes. :-)
:-) Eva

Eva Mihalik, February 28 at 1:15am Report

I can't estimate because I was in the crowd; it was dense! BBC told hundreds of thousands. The locals was speaking about 2-4 million people in the bigger rallies.

Let me give you some additional feelings what I observed and liked. Before this events people I talked to was often kind of apologizing about Egypt. I missed the pride about being Egyptian. And it was wonderful to see their new pride. When I was out there with a friend, he told me he always had a feeling that he was in the wrong time at the wrong place and this was the first time in his life where he felt he was in the right place at the right time. I had another friend, and when I asked him if he wanted to come there he told he could not bear the crowd, he never even went to soccer matches because of it (Egyptians are passionate about soccer!) But after the first time he went out you could not hold him back, he went every day, and came home so enthusiastic. :-)

After the victory you could see kids and teenagers in groups on the street cleaning up and refreshing the painting at the side of the main roads and painting the Egyptian tricolor on the trunk of the trees lining the street. :-) I hope I'm not getting boring. But it was something I have never seen in my entire life. This peaceful revolution (from the part of protesters) and still very determined, dissolving all religious, age, financial and other differences and bringing a new pride to the people. And hope. :-)
:-) Eva

Take a Drug (Prelude to the fall of a culture; in which "When all you have is a hammer, everything looks like a nail.")

Wearing a frown?
Take a drug.
Can't keep it down?
Take a drug.
Head hurts?
Take a drug.
Energy in spurts?
Take a drug.
Too much energy?
Take a drug.
Want more synergy?
Take a drug.
Feeling too happy?
Take a drug.
Feeling sappy?
Take a drug.
Too contentious?
Take a drug.
Feeling licentious?
Take a drug.
Can't get to sleep?
Take a drug.
Thinking too deep?
Take a drug.
Feeling tired?
Take a drug
Feeling wired?

Take a drug.
Kids bugging you?
Give 'em drugs;
won't study in school?
Give 'em drugs.
Can't get wet?
Take a drug.
Lost a bet?
Take a drug.
Feeling nervous?
Take a drug.
Can't get service?
Take a drug.
Can't stay dry?
Take a drug.
Wanna get high?
Take a drug.
Feeling antsy?
Take a drug.
Not enough fantasy?
Take a drug.
Can't stay sober?
Take a drug.
Feeling hungover?
Take a drug.
Can't stop talking?
Take a drug.
Problems walking?
Take a drug.
Can't get it up?
Take a drug.
Still can't shtupp?

Take a drug.
Can't talk to people?
Take a drug.
Feeling too anal?
Take a drug.
Nose feels itchy?
Take a drug.
Feeling bitchy?
Take a drug.
Peeing too much?
Take a drug.
Losing touch?
Take a drug.
Cannot pee?
Take a drug.
Feel too free?
Take a drug.
Got an erection lasting more than four hours?
Call a hooker. (Wait. What? . . .)
Take a drug.
Scared of heights?
Take a drug.
Can't sleep nights?
Take a drug.
Can't lose weight?
Take a drug.
Can't get a date?
Take a drug.
Feeling too skinny?
Take a drug.
Think you're a ninny?
Take a drug.

All worked up?
Take a drug.
Want to blow things up?
Take a drug.
Got a cough?
Take a drug.
Can't get off?
Take a drug.
Feeling too calm?
Take a drug.
Don't want to be a mom?
Take a drug.
Can't eat food?
Take a drug.
Gotta get nude?
Take a drug.
Eating too much?
Take a drug.
Out of touch?
Take a drug.
Feeling snappy?
Take a drug.
Too damn happy?
Take a drug.

t's a wonder we don't rattle when we dance.
For that matter, it's a wonder that we dance at all.

--Graves 2/17/18

Glossary:
Shtupp (Yiddish): To engage in coitus.

Terrorist

The cat watches birds.
As long as he stays inside
we have no dispute.

--Graves 3/10/11

The Evil White Male

I am the Evil, White Male.

I am the media-created creature of sly leer
said to peer cunningly from behind
every concealing bush, watching
for nefarious opportunity.

I am the maddening cape
employed by the Matador
to provoke the enraged, senseless
attack. The unreasoned

charge, in the direction
of the waiting blade.

I am the easy shot.

Stereotypically, I am named as
the sole reason for
the downfall of Earth.
I am the assigned cause of
The pollution of the soil.
The melting icecaps.
The oppression of (fill in the blank with whatever is
popular this week).

To the tabloid-minded, I am the

single cause
of wars, murder and tumult.
I am the convenient target, favored by
depthless investigation.

I am The Evil White Male.

I work.
I produce.
I strive to leave
a better world for my children.
I sweat.
I swear.
I pray.
I party.
I think.
I dream.
I make a paycheck, and
I pay my bills.

I carry my share of the load.

I am The Evil White Male!

"But Hitler was white!"

"Mussolini was white!"

"Stalin was white!"

"Genghis Kahn was... well, he wasn't
white -- but he could have been!
Evil! All of them, Evil!"

I am ten million farmers who grow your food.
I am a billion fathers who love their children, and who would die
for them.

I take your hand
and help you to rise
as you take mine and do the same.

I am The Evil White Male!

I am a maddening cape
employed by the Matador
to taunt you into unreasoned attack.
Into a senseless running charge
Full-on, into the
poised blade.

You - not I - are the real target.

We are children of the same Earth.
Evil eclipses hues and genders.

I require neither your condescension,
your derision, nor your condemnation.

Enough of this bullshit!   --Graves 8/18/17

The Fixed Game

I haven't played much poker.
I know people who have
and they tell me that
there is a pattern to a fixed game.
A free game is random
based on odds and
chance.

You win some, you lose some.
And if you understand the odds
you win more.

In a fixed game
if you pay attention
you'll notice a pattern.
You'll win some hands, but
in the long game, the House
always
wins.

If you see a pattern like this
you stop playing the game.
If you're playing with the
wrong crowd, trying to leave the game
might get you killed.

A fixed game only works, if the trusting patsy
never discovers that it's fixed. And
just keeps on playing. Hoping
to win.

In a fixed game, if you pay attention
you'll notice a pattern.

Bush, G. H. W.
Clinton, B.
Clinton. B.
Bush, G. W.
Bush, G. W.
Obama, B.
Obama, B.

I'm not saying that the game is fixed. But
it doesn't feel like we're playing a straight game
of "We the People . . ."

                    --Graves 4/4/14

The Gardener

Above all
she is patient.

Gardening
takes patience.
Her best friend
is her ghillie suit.
Not what you would think
to see her
at work.

She carefully studies the landscape
to make certain:
That the cut will be
perfect.
That the cut will serve
her purpose
That the cut will not
have to be repeated.

Then, she waits
for exactly
the right time
to prune. Breathing slowly
in/out.

She moves with deliberation
knowing that she will only get one
chance
to make the perfect cut.

Slowly
she makes
her
way
between the weeds.
Carefully
so as not to disturb the environment
in any way.

Then she waits.

She waits
for the turning of the Earth
to bring all of the elements into alignment.
The season
the day
the wind
the colors
the light.

All must be balanced.
All must be right.
She will only get one
chance.

She cuts.

A single gentle, guided move
of one finger.

A red bloom
blossoms
in the sun.

Red petals fall
to earth.

              --Graves 2/4/16

Definition: Ghillie suit (noun): A type of coverall, covered in torn cloth shreds, whose purpose is to blend in with background elements in the field. Typically worn by military snipers.

Etymology: As worn by ghillies, Scottish hunting guides and game wardens, in the 19th Century.

The Hatred of the Rich

Why hate the rich?
You might as well hate
the oil in a frying pan
for dimpling when you
finally get it hot enough to throw
a thick, delicious New York steak on it.

The rich have a tendency
to support the arts; to
engage in philanthropy
and to leave big tips!

Sure, some are snotty and supercilious.
Some are gracious, too.
Some of the snottiest people I've met
were on entitlement and were
snotty because they felt entitled.
No reason to hate them, either.
It's more a mental orientation than
an attitude dictated by economic condition.

You can resent people with money or
you can make your own.
You can be upset about
others with opportunity or
make your own.
There will always be people
happier than you, at any particular moment.

Thinking of ways to hold them back
is a waste of the time in which you
could be pushing yourself forward.

Their success does not
take away from your own.
Their happiness does not
take away from your own
unless you allow it.

Resentment is an emotion which kills you
and no one else.
It's a stupid pursuit.

Set out to make yourself happy.
Wish others well.
Lift yourself up, instead
of dragging yourself down.
What are you?
A mushroom?

--Graves 6/12/15

Notes:

Entitlement (noun): A term for government-sponsored programs which guarantee access to certain benefits by members of specific groups. They come into existence as a result of the activities of politicians. Said programs should be judged on their individual merits and might be deemed useful or harmful depending on the point of view of the citizen.

Metaphorical Note: A mushroom is a fungus which depends for its life on dead and dying organic material rather than actively generating its own energy from sunlight.

The Owl

The owl is fierce
and hunts in the night.
His cry shatters darkness
and inspires fright.
And nothing
that scurries
shall escape his sight.

                --Graves 9/2012

They Went

They were not perfect men
or women.
But they went.
They had flaws.
They were not all fighting
for our freedom.
But they went.
And many
did not return.

Some were jerks.
Some were assholes.
Some were angels.
And they went.

And when they returned,
some had families;
some had lives;
many had nothing.

But they went.

They took their place on the line
so that others would not have to.

If I could, I would shake
the hand of each of them.
Because they went.
But I cannot.   --Graves 5/27/13

TV Newscasters

Beware the person who, for
pay, takes an incident, written
in blood, and smears it, thickly
across your face
to make you think
that the world is a dark and
dismal place, coming
apart at its leaky seams.
And is not worth saving.
When just around the corner
bathed in light
crocuses bloom
and children delight
in the wonder of watching
bugs, and in bubbles floating
on the wind.
It is a new day.
It is a new world!
Embrace it!
Revel in it!

                    --Graves 4/23/21

We Should be More Than Just Entertainment

In a broad sense
we should be more than just
entertainment.

More than figures in the Colosseum arena
– scripted parts carelessly assigned.
Movements and motions pre-blocked. Fighting
each other, to the satisfaction
of those with seats.

More than chess-piece factions
warring over inconsequentially
pretentious trinkets.

It is the nature of that being, which
in this state, is pretending
to be human, that
we should be so much more.

More than anxious marionettes, engaged
in games, the outcome of which
was always just part of the plan.

More than the grotesque matador
who struts and waves the scarlet cape
tumescent with false accomplishment
as he dances in the bullfight ring.
The crowd, like vampires
drawing life from his
pretentious masquerade
the outcome of which is always prearranged.

We should be more than this.

More than bread and circuses for
those with seats. We should be
more than just entertainment.

It is the nature of that being
which in this state
is pretending to be human
that we should be so much more.

We should be more than
ballerinas frantically dancing on our toes, trying
to please those who would just as soon
see us broken and crawling.

We should be more than entertainment.

    --Graves 5/16/21

Notes:

"Blocking" (pre-blocked) is a theatrical term which refers to the precise, planned movement and positioning of actors on a stage in order to facilitate the performance of a play, ballet, film or opera.

On Poetry and Social Responsibility

Poetry is one of the most dangerous, most powerful, and one of the most unorganized forces in the world.

Consider the effect that a single poet can create on the human psyche.

Shakespeare, Rumi, Rimbaud, Dylan, Poe, Pound, Dickinson, Baudelaire, Cummings, Neruda, Yeats, Plath, Ginsberg, Burns, Bukowski, Dylan Thomas, Blake, Frost, Wordsworth, Whitman, and countless others.

Poetry combined with music was powerful enough to play an important part in helping to change the social face of my country in the 1960's. If you were there to witness it, you know exactly what I mean. One of the most famous pieces of poetry of that decade begins: "How many roads must a man walk down/before you call him a man..."

Poetry soothes the aching heart. It kindles the flame of love. It is a precursor to inspiration. It calls men to sail a sea that they otherwise might not. Poetry performs a catalytic function between conditions: a bridge between disassociation and engagement; between non-involvement and responsibility; between denial and consideration.

At some point, a piece of poetry left a mark on you that was indelible. You still can recall it. That quality in poetry can bring change to the world – literally.

If poetry is not also used to bring about needed change in social and political conditions, it denies a fundamental aspect of its basic purpose, and to this degree and in this way, it lies fallow.

Poetry is not bound by physical barriers. It is not stopped by walls. It can infiltrate elitist compounds, and pierce the walls of fortresses and prisons. It can bypass embargoes as easily as a breeze travels down a city street. I am writing from a redwood forest in California. You are reading this. Distance is not a barrier to poetry.

One of the reasons that poets are held in contempt by those who use force to suppress, is that while poets command the very, very real skills to inflame the spirit of those who are oppressed and move them to active social change or even open, violent revolt; that ability is far too often used by poets for nothing beyond introverted maunderings, voiced in cautious, hushed, whiny tones. As a result, suppressors find spitting on poets a very safe thing to do.

Poetry is powered by the human spirit. It is carried in the hearts and minds of the people. Historically, ideas have toppled empires. All social movements – all of the changes in history – have been sparked by communication.

"... I am the song on the lips
of slaves.

I am sire to the million whispers in the night;
before the riotous dawn.

I am the throbbing life blood;
the hope that breathes yet, beneath the heel
of the iron boot.
And awaits its time.

And I am that time
which *will* come.

I am the driver of men, beyond broad, deadly
expanses, thirsting
for new worlds.

I am the line
plotted past the edge of charts.

I am the dreams beyond those
yet dreamed.

I am the new voice of songs yet
to be formed on the lips of
those yet to be born.

And I am the dawn
of a new Age..."

Poetry once lacked the proper distribution system. We now have a distribution system which is more powerful than any in the history of Earth – the Internet. Change can now potentially take place "one reader at a time" on a very, very broad scale. Poetry does not need to sway six billion people in order to achieve its goal. It only has to reach and affect those with significant influence, or reach a significant number of people, for change to occur.

What if we had a million poets creating life-changing pieces in a wave which is directed at a single point of oppression? Or directed at a focused, few points of suppression? Think about it. What kind of effect might we then create?

It is time to send the tyrants screaming into the night, pursued by a wave of voices that no number of bullets can ever kill.

Poetry can change the world. But only if it is wielded, not proffered. Get organized. Pass it on.

"Night Must Fall on the Regime"

The time has come.

Night must fall on the regime.

You, whose proper function is to serve.

You, who turn your country on the roasting spit of oppression,
charring humanity to black flakes over
the painful fires of violence; seasoned
with the smell of fear.

This is *not* the way of humanity!

You do *not* speak for me!

You could once commit your perverted crimes
shrouded in secrecy.
But now, worldwide
awareness of your atrocities is just a URL click away.

The video taken with the phone of
the man in the street – upon whose neck
you once could stand with impunity
– and posted to the web, makes
secrecy no longer your option.
No longer your shield.

To sit silent and do nothing while you continue,
degrades me
and stains each of my brothers and sisters with shame.

To permit you to persist, reduces the humanity of each one
of the inhabitants of Earth.

Each one.

This is NOT the way of a leader.

This is *not* the way of humanity.

A populace is NOT your collection of personal toys
to be played with, and bled!
You pathetic, wanton child!
There is no pride in this.
Only decrepitude.

Stalin was thus.
Hitler was thus.
George III was thus.
The Masters of the Inquisition were thus.
These are your brothers-in-spirit.

If the only reasoning that you will respond to
is a knife at your throat,
then consider that you are now on notice.

Your lies and deceit will birth the bloody tumult.

I weep for your countrymen.
I weep for my brothers and sisters.

It is time.

Night must fall on the regime.

I am the poet.
And I live in a billion minds.
We are the dreamers of dreams.

And we will prevail.

Your remains will blow away on the fresh winds of morning
before the rising sun of a new day.

There are a million voices waiting to take my place.
A million songs being honed.
A sky-full of razor-sharp arrows that are all aimed at your heart.

Our songs live in the minds of your people.
Our songs form the million whispers in the night
before the riotous dawn.

Our songs feed the throbbing life-blood of hope
that breathes yet beneath the heel of the iron boot.
Awaiting its time.

And that time has come.

For the sake of humanity.
For the sake of songs yet to be formed
on the lips of those yet to be born.

Night will fall on the regime.

You cannot dull my advance.
Your suppression only sharpens
my quill and broadens my legend.

We live as one unturnable wave of forward motion.

And we speak for humanity.

We will outlive you.
We will outlast you.
You who would crush all hope.

You are my enemy.
This is personal.

I am the singer of songs.
I am the dreamer of dreams.
My brothers and sisters and I inspire the future, and craft
the inspirational blade that even now thirsts for your throat.
There are more poets on Earth than you can count.
And more than you can ever crush.

You cannot stop us.

The time has come.
Night *will*
fall on the regime.

–Graves 2/11/15

Poet's Note: Though this piece was originally written about poetry, its premise applies to all forms of art and the artists that power them. We are all in an unprecedented position to influence not only our culture, but the combined cultures of the planet. And who better to do it? Politicians have been wearing this hat for millennia and have driven themselves as a group into a generally distrusted and despised condition of existence. It is only fitting that we, as artists, bypass and handle. Not as those who would govern the culture, but as those who illustrate the direction that a culture should properly take in its evolution from the existing scene to a more ideal scene, and provide effective encouragement and motivation for the achievement of that evolution. As artists, its our job and should be our united purpose.

WRITING - POETRY

Poetic Convergence

Poetry should not
simply be the act of
finding words that rhyme
and placing them in measured lines
any more than sex should be
the monotonous, repetitive rubbing
together of skin
in the dark.

Words mingle like potential
lovers in festival masks
considering convergence.

Lacking direction, they mill about
forming lame conversation and
desperate small talk
hoping for more. Looking
for meaningful (or not) conjunction.
For counterpoint, wrapping
hungrily one around the other
in penetrating juxtaposition
shuddering alliteration.
Yearning for the onomatopoeic concatenation of
sounds
which in the end, fill the room, and hang
in the mind.

Words are sounds, rolled back
and forth on the warm
slippery, surface of the minds tongue.
Moved and molded
again and again, until
ready to be entered
on the page.

The best arrangements are rarely
predictable.

Twist them until they scream
with delight.
Tweak them until their meaning is
rigid and undeniable.
Take them, and travel to a place of wonder, because
cliche is so
humdrum-predictable. The steady
rhythm of a dull saw, that
puts
you
to sleep.

No life.

No excitement.
No spice. No tightening
gasp of delight
in the mind, at a glimpse of something
hoped for. A door
that opens into a wondrous new place
of transcendent ecstasy. A glimpse
of the holy vision.

When poetry causes the mind to catch its breath
then, it is working.

                    --Graves 11/22/12

Sequential Glossary:

Counterpoint: The technique of combining two or more melodic lines in such a way that they establish a harmonic relationship while retaining their linear individuality.

Juxtaposition: An act or instance of placing close together or side by side, especially for comparison or contrast.

Alliteration: The repetition of the same sounds, or of the same kinds of sounds at the beginning of words, or in stressed syllables, as in: "she sells sea shells by the seashore" or "oh! oh! oh! oh! Ohhhhh! Ohhhhh . . .". Modern alliteration predominantly involves consonants. Certain literary traditions, such as Old English verse, also alliterate using vowel sounds.

Onomotopoeiatic (from onomotopoeia): The naming of a thing or action by a vocal imitation of the sound associated with it (as buzz, hiss, smack, bang, bash, cuckoo, meow, honk, or boom).

Concatenation: A chain; a sequence of things or sounds related to, or dependent upon each other. Ex. "The concatenation of explosions from the string of firecrackers." Or "Like the concatenation of defensive soundbites following accusation in an election year."

Dull saw: A saw is an old saying or commonly repeated phrase or idea.

The Poet's Spell
(with apologies to the Bard, and to the three witches of Macbeth)

Fix the rubble, toil and trouble,
fire burn and cauldron bubble.
Stir the pictures bright and deep,
and from the fire they'll make the leap.
Into pixel, onto page,
dancing on the inner stage.

Words that cause from smoke uncurled,
the dreams of poets to be unfurled,
in radiant raiment shining bright;
visions that bend and twist the light.
Images that yearn with bliss,
like lovers lips that long for kiss.

Bring them here upon the page.
Bring them here to change the Age!
Or murmur softly songs that start
to stir the beating of the heart.
To flame the soul to heat of love
or cool the sadness lost thereof.

Bring them here to play their part.
Bring them here to gift my art
with clarity and strength of vision;
meanings lacking no precision.
Imagery and words which state,
that which I would communicate.

And I will take this piece and send
it on it's way new roads to wend.
Its purpose now to travel Earth
to soothe the sorrow, salve the dearth;
to lend its strength to those in need
to jog a mind, to plant a seed.

And if you will sweet Muse comply
and if to me the words will fly
I'll pen a piece to brighten the day
or through the dark, to show the way.
And if my words fulfill their role
they'll both inspire and heal the soul.

     --Graves 5/18/17

Glossary:

Thereof: From that cause or origin.
Wend: to proceed on (one's way)
Salve: Something which soothes or heals
dearth: A scarcity or lacking

On Writing Poetry:

When you write for yourself you can write whatever you want. It doesn't have to make sense to anyone but you. But when you write for others, that writing must contain truths that resonate with the public to which you are writing. They may not realize yet that these are truths, but these truths have to be there. They are what connects you to your readers. If you don't have that, you don't have shit.

--Graves 12/31/18

"today It is difficult to write"

Today sits poised on the brink of
something that I can't
quite

see.

Time fidgets

a snowman trying to melt
in preparation for the coming of summer
on a wintry, mid-December night.

Everything seems just out
of reach.

The idea of writing is fused with boredom
and anticipation throughout.
An unfocused wondering, about
which way to turn.

Rivers of words are glaciers
in the black, arctic night. Frozen
with dissatisfaction more than
anything.

Writing is simple.
It begins with decision.
Writing is a clean, crisp
crafting, of carvings.
Writing is simple.

Though, sometimes blocked
by "What for?"

Today is languid.
Life lingers on the street outside
and negotiates continuance with
any passing traffic willing to listen.
I can hear it
through my open window.

I am teetering here
on the edge
of Summer and Winter
trying not to fall
into a cotton-batting void
where no fire sparks the imagination with
the adrenaline spike that
I need, to vault into the next
tight, hot, wet, sweaty project.

To see with passion-glazed eyes
bright with painful creation.
Speeding down the mountain
through sweet, thieving air.
Racing the road ahead
past blurred, huge trees any of which
would dish out death as a favor
while looking, conveniently
the other way.

Speeding into the hot night
beneath the flapping wings of the tiny
erratic bat, who flies with crystal vision
born of a blindness
which is only apparent.

Seek not to be remembered for what
you have done. Seek instead
to ride forward on the ramifications of
your accomplishments.
For you will be back to ride
those rippling waves to shore.

No one
is eternal.
All are eternal, and in the
stone night none really sleep.
Dying is just a ruse to
confound spirits too bored to see
the repeating game.

I bathe in molten lava, cool to the touch
drenched in the passion of carving
out a universe in the pixels
of my touchstone to God
and the denizens who dwell
beyond the bounds of time
out beyond the click of the
clock -- knowing that the ravages of time
are only a masquerade
that we play to sample the lower emotions
that are - in our natural state - difficult to reach
because: Why should we?

The spirit flies, not needing to -- being everywhere at
once
and locating by choice only.
The rush, a contrived boost to the dismissal
of boredom from
the walls
of the castle, where I sit
thinking
about
things.

Because today,
it is difficult to write.

                --Graves 1/1/15

Regarding Editing

Once you understand writing;
never let ANYBODY edit your poetry.
Take their suggestions (if you want)
and walk 99.99 percent of them to
the trash, where they belong.

They don't share your vision.
They don't share your clarity.
If editors could write poetry,
they would.

Until you reach this point
- where you can write -
you may need a radical awakening
or two.

I did.

Life is exactly like this.

                    --Graves 1/24/22

Borders is Closing (A Saturday afternoon; and the passing of a friend.)

I will miss the smell of books.
Bound paper. Ink on a page.
And their coffee.

A place to sit, on Pacific Avenue
out of the rain
and write.

It was my version of
Hemingway's "clean, well-lighted place"
(without the despair, loneliness
or nihilistic taint.)

There is something that feels sacred
about a repository of books

for sale or not.

And Borders was one
of the places where
from time to time
I went to write, to peruse
and to wonder at
the thoughts of others.

Stacks of friends-in-paper
of like minds
or not.
A place to go, and touch pages.

To stand in the lighted space, and feel
smooth
paper beneath my fingertips.
And feel the words
of others
in my eyes.

It's not that I mind Amazon
or Kindle or Nook
and the like.
I've shopped the pixel places
but

there is something holy about
"the bookstore"
as an intersection of intellectual
pathways.
A nexus.
A springboard of
dimensional collaboration.

Its occupants were literate.
Thirsty for
words.
Capable of considering
the ideas of another in order to
reach the lofty places – the great open places in

their minds.
Or simply to scratch the itch
of curiosity.

I wonder if the Library at
Alexandria
was like that
before it was sacked.

                 -- Graves 10/18/14

Just Because

It's easy to write about grief.
About loss.
About some everyday personal crisis.
It's as easy as falling.
It's the easy shot.
The cheap seats.

Grief itself, as a subject
is a mundane
too-well-traveled poetic road.
The sights to see along the way
are published in cheap little
tri-fold brochures
for tourists to cram into their luggage
and throw away once they get home.

Weeping, after all, is not necessarily bad.
People weep
from loss, or from a feeling of relief.
People weep from pain or from a flood
of enhanced belief.

I'm not saying that poetry
should (necessarily) be about
the achingly beautiful songs
of soaring angels. Or
about massive, haunted, craggy formations
of glowing clouds in a bright
moonlit summer sky.
Or shimmering pastoral settings that
would make a saint weep with joy.
Or about the gritty street-life of the underbelly.

Far be it from me
to tell you
what to write.

It's my opinion.
Just because
it is.

Poetry's holy calling
is to stretch beyond the confines
of a comfortable mind.
To look beyond the trite
the mundane
the commonplace
except perhaps to expand it
by observation and recounting
into something remarkable.
To travel to that place beyond
sight. That place where
dreams play out as real.
Where thoughts rarely go.

To take the turn, around
that bend where the road
doesn't go.

Because it's poetry.

                      --Graves 8/7/20

On Writing - a note to Paul W. Morris Sr. in 2012

You mentioned that you once wanted to be a writer.

Writing is an interesting thing, Paul. It grabs you or it doesn't. Or it insinuates itself into your life until it becomes sort of a point of relief. A place where you can go, away from everything else, and create.

It's an art form that lends itself to many situations and forms -- from haiku to non-fiction to journalism to the great novels. All equally addictive for the writer, and each as valid as the other.

The act of writing doesn't require the formulation of a massive, complex plot, necessarily. But it does require the writer to write in his own voice (albeit through various characters at times) and from his own viewpoint and understanding of the world around him.

At its core, art itself is simply a quality of communication. I didn't come up with that definition, it's one that I learned from L. Ron Hubbard; an extremely successful writer, among other things. I have found it to be true regardless of the art form - music, writing, painting, cinematography - you name it.

So writing - as an art form - is communication. The quality is something that you as a writer develop, enhance, mold and hone. But it is yours. Your goal should not be to write like Shakespeare, or Hemingway, or Steinbeck or Dostoyevsky - necessarily - your goal should be to write as yourself.

Back in 1993, I wrote a note to myself: "There will always be someone younger and faster, there's sometimes someone smarter and more perceptive; there's never anyone with your viewpoint and perspective." And this is the way that I think a writer should regard writing.

You can start writing anything -- observations from working at the Point. Thoughts about people there, descriptions of the terrain, circumstances that you encounter. "Walden; or, Life in the Woods" details Henry David Thoreau's experiences over the course of two years, two months and two days, in a cabin he built near Walden Pond, in Connecticut.

Do not write and edit at the same time. Write. Get the stuff out of your head, and then go back and tweak, rewrite, cut, add, etc. Unless one is merciless in the editing, everything suffers. Never fall in love with a passage, image or clever turn of words to the point that it becomes a detriment to the overall piece -- you'll know what I mean when you run into this. There have been many times when - in the final editing of a poem, I've cut whole verses or descriptive passages out of a piece because they distracted from the flow of the piece or pulled the reader of on a needless tangent, or because they were just there because they were clever.

Save the stuff that you cut. It may be the jumping off point for a later piece. Happens to me all the time.

I (used to) read Esquire (in 2012 and earlier, before they changed editors and shifted their attention to "being fashionable") for their use of words. It was very much worth reading; but I rarely - very rarely - read the poetry of others. It has a tendency to affect my writing voice. I research my pieces pretty extensively, but only to the degree that's needed for the piece. Research, while a good thing to do, should not turn into a vacation from writing for any longer than necessary. Read to see what others have done. To learn about economy in the use of words, about styles of communication, about the use of viewpoint, etc. But write in your own voice. Kerouac is an excellent (and extreme) example of writer using his own voice. In painting, Monet and Van Gogh are examples.

Another point that Hubbard made, is that "... a writer WRITES." So if you want to write, write. Get better at it, and write some more. That's how most writers turn into good writers, I think.

Best of luck! Break a leg and all that, my friend! :-)

--Graves 10/10/20

Something that Rhymes - On the "Importance" of Rhyming

As a poet it's bugged me, the number of times
 that I've searched and I've searched for the right word that rhymes
with something I felt that I just had to say
and that had to be said, in a "poetic" way.

Use the wrong word, and it simply unwinds
the verse being written - by stealing its spine.
It simply won't work, and just won't align,
with the way it should read, like something that rhymes.

If the word is too trite or simply not right
for the phrase or the line, or just not quite bright
I'll scratch the thing out, toss the page in the trash
'Cause a single wrong word turns the poem into hash.

Not rhyming in poetry's surely no crime.
Consider free verse
or haiku,
not a rhyme
in the whole blinkin' bunch
just pacing
and time,
and exquisite expressions
but nary a
rhyme.

It has to sound easy while packing a punch.
Without arcane reference (that sounds out to lunch).
I'd trade out my soul, be it oh so sublime.
If only dear God you'd just give me a rhyme!

                    --Graves 11/21/20

The Poet

I am the poet. I live
the holy nightmare.
I travel the ecstatic transition.

For me, the light bends differently.
The rainbow radiates a vibrant symphony
in the key of red-orange
or some other hue.

Magnificent choirs resound from within
the vast tumble of clouds, hanging
in the morning sky, changing
with the shifting light; harmonically sifting
the colors as the sun rises and echoes
brilliantly off the far mountains.

I am the poet. Verse grows
within me, pulsating with life.
Greedy for its own existence.
And forth it comes, skipping gaily or
strutting murderously, as I
in sweet agony of creation, give birth.

I am the poet. A blink
in the wrong direction takes me
to places which are not earthen lands, but
vistas where hope is a particular shade of light.
And rage is a cool breeze on an autumn
afternoon under blazing, red flames of dead leaves.

I am the poet. I see
divinity in snowflakes, and civility
in blood-red rivers of rebellion.

I throb yet, from a love a thousand years past.
And your hot breath across my throat
still haunts me.
And burns.

I am the poet. The ordinary
and the fantastic sit side by side at a table
in a falling raindrop.

A lifetime is lived in a pointed blade
of grass that floats for a moment
on the wind, and then
rushes downstream to rot
on some foreign
shore.

There, to begin again.

                      –Graves 6/30/17

A Poet's Wish

A life in service of the Muse
spent planting dust from imaginary stars
in fecund, conceptual earth
from which grows poetry; like the
twisting vines of clustered, climbing roses.

For that, it seems
is pretty much how it's done.

A life in which passion's burning blood
is the most tepid to which
one aspires. And from that blood
fall drops of glowing fire
along the winding road. Spots of light

to guide a traveler
too long locked in search.
Spots of light for me to follow
on that darkest night, and find
my own way home.

A life which ends in
sunset spilt like shining blood
on western skies.
A night which with her cool
sparkling blessing bids
both farewell to one
and joyous welcome
to another day.   –Graves 7/10/21

www.ingramcontent.com/pod-product-compliance
Lightning Source LLC
Chambersburg PA
CBHW020159170426
43199CB00010B/1112